ONE HEART, ONE FLESH,

One Love

ONE HEART, ONE FLESH,

One Love

DIANE HAMPTON

W

WHITAKER
HOUSE

ONE HEART, ONE FLESH, ONE LOVE: HOW TWO IMPERFECT PEOPLE CAN HAVE A PERFECT MARRIAGE
(previously titled *Imperfect Mates, Perfect Marriage* and *Excellence in Marriage*)

ISBN: 0-88368-573-6
Printed in the United States of America
© 1985 by Whitaker House
Whitaker House
30 Hunt Valley Circle
New Kensington, PA 15068
website: www.whitakerhouse.com

Library of Congress Cataloging-in-Publication Data
Hampton, Diane.
  [Imperfect mates, perfect marriage]
  One heart, one flesh, one love : how two imperfect people can have a perfect marriage / Diane Hampton.
    p. cm.
Previously published: Imperfect mates, perfect marriage. © 1985.
  ISBN 0-88368-573-6 (pbk.)
  1. Marriage. 2. Interpersonal relations. 3. Marriage—Religious aspects—Christianity. I. Title.
  HQ734.H2595 2003
  306.872—dc21   2003008413

1 2 3 4 5 6 7 8 9 10 11 12 / 09 08 07 06 05 04 03

Contents

Foreword

I wish I could tell you that our marriage has always been perfect and that our attitudes and concern for each other have always been above reproach. I wish I could say that harsh words and hurt feelings have never been a part of our lives. If I could honestly tell you that, then this book would probably never have been written.

The excellent marriage that Diane and I have today did not come easily. We are distinct individuals with our own personalities, habits, likes, and dislikes. If we had not discovered more in life than just ourselves, our marriage could have failed as so many others have. We praise God for His wisdom that has enabled us to change our lives—wisdom that has transformed our marriage and kept it strong.

Throughout this book, Diane opens her heart and soul to share personal experiences similar to your own. The principles she teaches are founded on God's Word.

Since God is no respecter of persons, you, too, can receive all the rewards we have received. May this book be a blessing to your marriage!

—Don A. Hampton

Introduction

*L*ove never fails" (1 Corinthians 13:8 NKJV). Of course it doesn't! As the Bible teaches,

> *Love is very patient and kind, never jealous or envious, never boastful or proud, never haughty or selfish or rude. Love does not demand its own way. It is not irritable or touchy. It does not hold grudges and will hardly even notice when others do it wrong.* (verses 4–5 TLB)

I could get along just fine with *love*. It's my husband that I need help with. Unfortunately, my husband is not always very patient and kind. He occasionally exhibits jealousy and has been known to be selfish and rude. There are times when he demands his own way. And when he hasn't eaten, you should see how irritable and touchy he can get! As a rule, he doesn't hold grudges, but it would be ludicrous to suggest that he seldom notices when others do him wrong.

If you are married to *love,* this book will be of little value to you. If, however, you happen to be married to an imperfect mate, as I am—or if you are willing to admit to being imperfect yourself, as I am—then this book will be of help to you.

It's difficult enough to try to make a marriage wonderful when you are not married to *love.* But when he is not married to *love* either, it can get really tricky.

I am not a professor or a psychologist, but I have had my "MRS. degree" for more than thirty years. The greatest recommendation I can give myself, since I have no impressive credentials to offer, is that although my husband and I are both imperfect mates, we are wonderfully happy together. I still delight in our relationship, and I have reason to believe that he does, too.

If you are willing to spend the time reading, I am willing to share some of this hard-earned knowledge with you. I'm going to skip over the platitudes and get down to the nitty-gritty. I will be quoting liberally from the Scriptures because I have found them to be the most practical and helpful source in dealing with imperfect mates.

Your Marital Heart

What a learning experience marriage is! What a testing ground! At its worst, you learn more in one year of marriage than in fifteen years of any other relationship. At its best, you begin to become what God intended you to be. You grow and help to shape one another as nothing else can. You learn what you are made of, you learn what God is made of, and you learn what love is made of.

In every marriage, there is a part I like to call the heart of the marriage. It serves much the same function as your physical heart. Your physical heart is constantly taking in the old, deoxygenated blood, which is full of useless waste, and pumping out fresh blood that is full of life-giving oxygen.

Your marital heart is also constantly taking in the tired daily routines of married life and pumping out fresh, revitalized love. When the heart of your marriage is free from obstructions, you can make it through seemingly impossible circumstances.

The past thirty years and two children have created some struggles in our marriage. But when my heart is right, problems don't seem as big, and bad habits don't seem as irritating. Part of this book contains the valuable principles God has shown me about keeping my heart right before Him.

Two are better than one; because they have a good reward for their labour. For if they fall, the one will lift up his fellow....Again, if two lie together, then they have heat: but how can one be warm alone? And if one prevail against him, two shall withstand him; and a threefold cord is not quickly broken. (Ecclesiastes 4:9–12)

I have tremendous respect for God's plan for marriage and the family. May these pages help you and your imperfect mate build a marriage of perfection—one heart, one flesh, one love.

Storing Treasures 1

God has taught me a powerful principle that is one of the keys to a happy, fulfilling marriage. This principle concerns the treasures we store in our hearts.

Jesus taught a great deal about the care and tending of the heart. He said, *"A good man* [or woman] *out of the good treasure of the heart bringeth forth good things"* (Matthew 12:35).

The dictionary defines *treasure* as "something to value greatly or to cherish for future use." It is "accumulated or stored wealth." Notice that a treasure is not for now, but it is something put away for the future.

Jesus said that from the good treasures in our hearts, from the stored wealth put away for future use, we bring forth good things.

We know from Scripture that this was one of the attributes that Mary, the mother of Jesus, had. She knew how to store treasures in her heart. The Bible tells us, *"Mary kept all these things, and pondered them in her heart"* (Luke 2:19).

God showed me that I needed to develop this quality in my marriage. Let me give you a few examples of "treasures" that I have stored in my heart with regard to my husband. These are everyday experiences from our lives—the kind of experiences on which a marriage is built. They may not seem like treasures to you, but they are priceless to me!

The Rescue

Several years ago, my father, whom I loved very much, had terminal cancer. At one point, he was bedridden, and I was needed in Chicago for a few days to take care of him. That meant I had to drive from St. Louis to Chicago with our daughter, Heather, who was five. I had never taken such a long trip by car without my husband before.

At this same time, we were in the midst of a big rape scare in St. Louis. Every day the newspaper had frightening headlines. The banks were even giving out "Send Help" signs for women who might be stranded in their cars. That year I was

Safety Chairman of our school PTA, and we had arranged to show a police department film dealing with rape. All this was very much on my mind as my daughter and I started out on our long trip.

About halfway to Chicago, in a desolate area of Illinois, my heart dropped as *"the thing which I greatly feared"* (Job 3:25) came upon me. The "hot light" glared at me from the dash as I pulled over to the side of the road.

It was a bitterly cold, windy October afternoon. We had left for Chicago directly after church, so my daughter and I were dressed in our Sunday clothes. I can still remember how cold I was in my heels and lightweight coat as I opened the hood of the car.

When I saw the "hot light," I thought the radiator must need water. "Praise God!" I said to myself. "I have some water in a bottle in the car. I'll just pour some in the radiator."

As any man will tell you, a little knowledge and a woman with a car can be a dangerous combination. I opened what I thought was the radiator because it had a screw cap. It didn't look exactly like other radiators I had seen, but it was a new car, and I thought they had changed the design. I poured the water in with all the confidence of someone who doesn't know what she is doing. Relieved that I had taken care of things, I happily got back into the car and tried to start the engine again, but the "hot light" was still on.

Frankly, at this point, my spirits began to sag. But being basically optimistic by nature and confident in the care of my heavenly Father, I began to pray. At the same time, I tried to keep my mind off what could happen to a woman and a child stranded alone on the highway.

Eventually, a man and his young son stopped to help. As he looked under the hood to try to diagnose the problem, I explained how I had poured water into the "radiator." He then explained that I had poured water into the crank case—not the radiator.

I was devastated and sure I had ruined the engine in my brand new car.

The man said that it would be all right to drive for a few miles, even with the temperature gauge reading hot. He followed me to a service station a few miles ahead where a huge sign read, "Open Twenty-four Hours—Mechanic on Duty." Relief flooded me as I thanked God and thanked the man who had stopped to help. Feeling that he was leaving us in good hands, he continued on his way.

By this time, it was late afternoon, and my daughter and I were chilled to the bone. We headed for the warmth of the station only to discover that their heat was not working. Not only was the heat not working, but the mechanic was not working. In fact, there was no mechanic on duty at all. Furthermore, there was no mechanic in the whole town! Not only was there no mechanic, but the station did not stay open twenty-four hours at all; they closed at six on Sundays!

I would like to report that, as a mighty woman of faith, I was unmoved by the circumstances. However, in truth, I was beginning to feel desperate. To make matters worse, the station attendants ignored us completely except to inform us that they would close soon.

I called my father in Chicago to let him know what had happened, but, of course, there was nothing he could do. I knew that Don wasn't home, because we had discussed his plans to take our oldest daughter skating that afternoon. Thankfully, I did know how to reach him. As I searched for the coins to make the toll call, I realized I had used up the last of my change in calling my father.

It is still hard for me to understand how uncaring the service station attendants were. When I took a bill and asked for change for the phone, they refused, saying they needed their change for their customers.

In my whole life, I don't believe I have ever felt so alone and so vulnerable. In tears, I called a neighbor collect and asked her to reach Don for me. More quickly than I dared to hope, the phone rang.

When I heard Don's voice, I felt as if I had gotten hold of John Wayne and all the U.S. Cavalry! Fifteen years of knowing him and knowing what kind of a man he was came flooding up inside me. I knew he would drop everything and come for us in a second. That sure knowledge and the memory of it on one of the worst days of my life has become a treasure I have stored in my heart over the years.

To this day, I am in awe of how much help he was—even over the telephone. He comforted me, consoled me, and knew just what to do.

Sometimes now when he does something that is not so wonderful, when he lets me down, as we all do to one another at times, I go to the treasure—to the accumulated wealth stored in my heart—and it sustains me. It sustains our love, and it sustains the precious heart of our marriage.

Memorized Moments

Another treasure I store in my heart about Don is a sweet, romantic gesture I have never forgotten. At one time, I sewed a great deal. One winter, I decided to make a winter coat for myself.

I almost got cold feet when I saw the expensive price of the fabric. What if I made a mistake and ruined it? I would still have no winter coat, yet all my available funds would be depleted.

But Don encouraged me, so I began. What a project! I worked and worked on it. One day, as I was finally getting near the end, Don called from work and asked how the coat was coming. I told him that I was just putting in the hem. We talked for a little while and then hung up.

That evening when he came home from work, he handed me a beautiful, gift-wrapped package from Neiman Marcus. When I opened it, I found the most beautiful black nightgown I had ever seen.

He said, "That's for wives who make their own winter coats." This was so unexpected that tears came to my eyes. It made me feel so special. Don's thoughtfulness on that occasion became a treasure I have stored in my heart, a precious memory I put away for future use.

When Don says something that is not so wonderful—and we all do at times—I go to the treasures stored in my heart, and they sustain me.

The apostle Paul put it this way in Philippians 4:8:

Whatsoever things are true, whatsoever things are honest, whatsoever things are

*just, whatsoever things are pure, whatso-
ever things are lovely, whatsoever things
are of good report; if there be any virtue,
and if there be any praise, think on these
things.*

Storing treasures in your heart is not a natural tendency, but you can develop it with God's
help. Take a few moments, and think back over
your married life. You should find many treasures stored there.

Another way of expressing this vital principle from God's Word was contained in a popular song of a few years ago. It made mention of
"memorizing moments that I'm fondest of." Later,
the singer says that his "cup runneth over with
love." Storing treasures will help keep your marital cup running over with love, too.

This is not just some fuzzy-headed ideal that
Paul thought up; it is a vital part of a strong
marriage! You see, your heart shows. One of the
most foolish things I ever believed was that my
husband couldn't sense my heart. I thought that
if I acted a certain way, that would be enough.
How wrong I was. A man senses a woman's
heart.

I can talk with a man or woman for thirty
minutes and get a good idea of what is filling his
or her heart. If I can discern so much in a total
stranger from a few moments of conversation, how

much more can your marriage partner tell what is in your heart?

Out of the Abundance of the Heart

When a woman begins to store treasures and accumulate wealth in her heart, something amazing happens: her words change.

When you keep your heart full of good treasures, you don't have to watch your tongue. Jesus said, *"Out of the abundance of the heart the mouth speaketh"* (Matthew 12:34). Words of encouragement and appreciation come forth when your heart is full of good thoughts and precious memories. Like the virtuous woman of Proverbs 31, your tongue becomes *"the law of kindness"* (v. 26).

You can store good treasures in your heart, but the opposite is also true. Jesus said, *"An evil man* [or woman] *out of the evil treasure bringeth forth evil things"* (Matthew 12:35). You can also accumulate evil treasures in your heart by dwelling on your husband's shortcomings, on the times he has embarrassed you, on his physical flaws, or on some other area in which he may have a weakness.

You can get to the place where you are living contrary to the Scripture. Your thoughts take on the following pattern: "If there be any fault, if there be any criticism, if there have been any disappointments, think on these things."

You don't have to spend much time thinking on these negative things before you discover what they can do to harm your marriage.

When you keep an itemized list of another's shortcomings (evil treasures), you have to watch your tongue! You have to guard every word, but you still get into trouble because *"the tongue can no man* [or woman] *tame"* (James 3:8).

If you are having trouble with your tongue, look to your heart! When your heart is not right, something inside you has to bring forth something evil. Your heart controls your words.

The opposite is also true. When your heart is full of good treasures, it is hard not to express them. When I was a young woman, I remember "falling in love" many times. One of the hardest things for me was not to tell the young man how I felt. I longed to say, "I love you. I think you are so wonderful."

Elizabeth Barrett Browning didn't have to watch her tongue. Can anyone doubt what was in her heart as she wrote the beautiful *Sonnets from the Portuguese* to her husband-to-be, Robert Browning? She penned,

How do I love thee? Let me count the ways.
I love thee to the depth and breadth and
   height
My soul can reach....

These words were written out of the abundance of her heart. It is interesting to note that during the period when most of her forty-four sonnets were written, Elizabeth's health dramatically improved! Just prior to her marriage, she was transformed from a semi-invalid to a vigorous woman.

Healing and restoration often result from a heart filled with good treasures.

Jesus said that out of the *"abundance of the heart,"* the mouth speaks. *Abundance* doesn't mean that you aren't mad at him anymore. *Abundance* means having more than an adequate supply. It comes from storing treasures, from dwelling on *"whatsoever things are good,"* and from "memorizing" moments that you're fondest of.

Outside Influences

I used to spend a lot of time with a group of friends whom I particularly enjoyed. But for a while, we couldn't seem to get together. Something would come up, or we would have conflicting plans. I began to sense God's hand in this, so I followed the leading in my spirit and backed off from seeing these women for a time.

After a number of months, we met for lunch again. We hadn't been together very long when I realized I was saying things that I didn't even believe! As the other women criticized their husbands, I heartily joined in and began finding fault with Don. I was tearing down rather than building up. Suddenly, it became clear that the Lord did not want me to be involved in such destructive conversation.

That experience taught me to choose my friends more carefully. Now all my friends and I have one thing in common: we build up our husbands! After having lunch with these wise women, I can come home full of love and new appreciation for my mate.

Proverbs 14:1 tells us, *"Every wise woman buildeth her house: but the foolish plucketh it down with her hands."* I've often thought that this Scripture could be paraphrased to say, "A foolish woman plucketh it down with her mouth."

Many people find it impossible to control their tongues because they start by trying to restrain their words. Jesus advised us to start with our hearts.

You can begin today to store treasures and to accumulate wealth in your heart regarding your husband. If your heart isn't full of treasures, it doesn't need to stay that way. It isn't spilled milk; it's just an empty cup!

Begin to memorize fond moments and store precious treasures, and you will quickly see the change it will make in your marriage. As Jesus promised, it will bring forth good things.

As you pray this prayer, let the Lord show you special incidents in your married life that you can store away.

Dear heavenly Father,

I want to have a heart filled with good treasures. Help me to be sensitive to the precious moments that pass through my life. Help me to dwell on the good things and to store them away for the future, so that my heart will run over with love. In Jesus' name, Amen.

Terrific Toughness

2

Your physical heart is surrounded by a thin but very tough lining called the pericardium. This lining protects the heart from rubbing against the lungs and the wall of the chest. The heart could be damaged and would be extremely vulnerable without this strong outer layer.

Your tender marital heart also needs to be surrounded by a tough outer layer. First Corinthians 13:4–8 lists the attributes of love. I particularly like the way one part is translated in the *Amplified Bible*. It says that love *"is not touchy"* (v. 5). The King James Version describes it this way: love *"is not easily provoked."* To be *"touchy"* is to be easily offended. A touchy person must be handled with caution or great tactfulness.

Most women are more emotional than their husbands, so we especially need to develop a tough outer layer around our marital hearts. I know women who spend days in emotional upheaval over some casual remark their husbands made or some imagined slight. This touchiness affects the building of strong emotional bonds in marriage.

Christians should be the hardest people in the world to offend. Jesus was a man of strong feeling. He wept openly, He was moved with compassion, and He rose up in righteous anger with great boldness. But He never brooded over offenses. He was not touchy or easily offended. He didn't require "expert handling."

My husband is in business with another fine Christian man. At the heart of their partnership is a genuine respect for each other's character. One of the reasons their partnership has remained healthy, strong, and mutually beneficial is their ability to strongly disagree without letting it affect the heart of their relationship.

On the outside of the heart of this partnership is a tough outer layer that allows freedom to exchange ideas and hash out differences. They can receive from one another without a constant need to weigh each word carefully. This kind of tough outer layer is also essential to a good marriage.

Open Rebuke

Having lost his mother as a child, my husband grew up in a male-dominated environment.

Believe me, he is not one to mince words. Over the years, however, I have come to love this quality of frankness in Don. The Bible says, *"Open rebuke is better than secret love. Faithful are the wounds of a friend"* (Proverbs 27:5–6). It also tells us that if we rebuke a *"wise man,"* he will love us (Proverbs 9:8).

You lose out on something good in marriage when you are too touchy or too easily offended to receive correction from your husband. Sometimes you need frank feedback. You're human, and you can get off track. Your mate is often in the best position to observe your life. If you pout for days over words that were true, though maybe not presented in the most tactful manner, he will not feel free to speak frankly to you again. Don may not always be tactful, but he is usually right on target.

A number of years ago, when my first book was published, I was invited to speak at many churches in our area. I was also in a leadership position at our church. Everyone was telling me how wonderful I was and how much I was being used of God—and I began to believe it!

One particular incident involved a church dinner to which everyone was to bring a casserole. Since I was in leadership in this particular group, I decided I was exempt from taking any food. Now, I didn't exactly put that thought into words, but my husband picked up the prideful attitude that was creeping into my heart.

As Don and I were driving to the dinner, he said to me, "Diane, that's just plain pride." It made me so angry when he said that. I reeled off several excuses, but the rebuke had already reached my spirit.

I knew he was right, and I was amazed at how easily a proud spirit had slipped into my heart.

Having a husband who is not hesitant to rebuke me when I need it has spared me much heartache. Although I may not like it at the time, Don knows I will not allow offense to set in. With his frankness and God's grace, I have learned this quality of "terrific toughness." It has helped me countless times.

Forgotten Birthdays

Most wives dream that their husbands will make a big celebration out of special days, and they should, but sometimes they just don't. Let's face it. We have, and are, imperfect mates.

Two women I know have husbands who forget their birthdays and other special occasions—with regularity! Both men love their wives and are thoughtful and considerate in other ways; but for some unknown reason, they often forget special days.

I have watched these women over a number of years. One woman allows each forgotten birthday to penetrate her heart. She drags around for days, and while she says little, her silence shouts. This woman is in the rut of "marital martyrdom."

The other woman hasn't been married as long. But she, too, soon discovered that her husband was not going to remember every special occasion as she had hoped. During the first years of their marriage, she was hurt by his forgetfulness. Anyone would be. But gradually, as time has gone by, I have seen her develop this "pericardium" around her heart. When her husband forgot a special occasion, she did not take it personally. Instead, she developed a sense of humor about it. "Well, he forgot my birthday again," she said. "I guess I will just have to go out and buy myself something wonderful."

These words were spoken with genuine good humor—not sarcasm. She developed a terrific toughness that would not allow resentment against her husband to take root in her heart. She made a decision that her love was not going to be touchy.

In recent years, I have seen this woman's husband remember special occasions more and more often. Why? Because *"love never fails"* (1 Corinthians 13:8 NKJV), and love *"is not touchy"* (v. 5 AMP).

Due Seasons and Piercing Swords

The world would be a better place if everyone communicated with greater skill and ability. Proverbs 15:23 says, *"A word spoken in due season, how good it is!"* How wonderful a word of encouragement is when you need it most.

The problem is that not all words are spoken *"in due season."* The world is filled with people who have trouble communicating well. They themselves are often frustrated by their lack of skill. Their words sometimes come at you like a piercing sword.

The same book that describes so beautifully *"a word spoken in due season"* acknowledges that *"there is one who speaks like the piercings of a sword"* (Proverbs 12:18 NKJV).

It is hard to keep from being offended by words. Sometimes just the tone in which something is said can be hurtful. But you have a choice. You can allow these words to enter your heart and spend a good part of your life recouping, or you can develop a "terrific toughness" that protects your tender heart.

I Don't Know Many Words of Praise

Women are generally more verbal than men. Men often have difficulty expressing all that is in their hearts. I find the song "Friendly Persuasion" very touching because it tenderly addresses this masculine trait. It says,

> Thee I love,
> Though I don't know many words of praise,
> Thee pleasures me in a hundred ways.

Here is a man who deeply loves this woman. She pleases him in a hundred ways, but he just can't seem to put it into words. When he tries to tell her, the words seem foolish and wrong. Listen to the rest of this song.

> Arms have I,
> Strong as an oak,
> For this occasion.
> Lips have I to kiss you, too,
> In friendly persuasion.

This man is expressing something precious, but his wife must learn to listen with her heart as well as her ears. Her husband's verbal skills may improve somewhat, but *he is probably never going to be able to say all the things she wants to hear*. If she can learn to listen with her heart, her cup will run over.

Before Don and I were married, an incident happened that illustrates this principle. We had just recently become engaged. One beautiful spring day, Don called and said he had bought something for me and wanted to bring it over. As a very romantic, prospective bride, I envisioned a music box that played "our song" or perhaps a necklace with some meaningful inscription that I would treasure forever.

My expectations were so great that anything he brought would probably not have lived up to them. But I was truly unprepared for the actual surprise. He proudly took me out to his beloved Chevy, opened the door, and displayed the seat belt he had just installed in the center seat position.

On the surface, this seemed as uninspired a gift as anyone could imagine. But if I had listened with my heart, I would have known that he was saying, "I am going to take care of you. I want to protect you. You are very valuable to me." It is the same feeling expressed in the song "Friendly Persuasion": "Arms have I, strong as an oak, for this occasion."

The positioning of the seat belt right next to him was Don's way of saying, "I want you close to me. I like the feeling of your body next to my body."

Don was expressing two of the qualities that I value so much in him today: deep commitment to take care of me and his desire to have me physically close to him. He wanted to tell me, "Thee pleasures me in a hundred ways," but the words were not there. So he bought this seat belt and spent his afternoon installing it.

Learn to develop this quality of listening with your heart. If you don't, you will miss many of your husband's deepest expressions of love.

Listening with Your Heart

Of all the husbands on the earth today, there are probably only a small percentage who are skilled at expressing what's in their innermost hearts.

I couldn't help being amused at a remark made after a marriage seminar I attended. One of the speakers gave an excellent lesson on the "need for good communication." Part of her talk was taken from two books that she recommended to the group—one was for the man and the other for the woman.

A couple of weeks after the classes, I happened to see one of the women who had also attended. She commented on how much she had enjoyed the seminar and the books. "But" she said, gesturing toward her nearby husband, "he just can't seem to get his part right!" This man was not some ignorant, backwoods hillbilly. He was a fine, respected professional.

Some men are never going to "get their part right," so the wife has a choice to make. She can choose to constantly feel let down and deprived, or she can learn to listen with her heart.

God created some men with the ability to operate on the brain with exacting precision. Others can maneuver huge machines with skill and competence or take a broken-down car and make it work perfectly. But for every man who can't put into words all that is in his heart, God created a woman—a helpmeet—with the ability to listen with her heart.

Women are born with this ability in varying degrees, but not all wives develop it. A sweaty child, flushed with the excitement of a summer day, can bring a handful of crudely picked wildflowers in a grimy little fist, and a mother will be moved to tears by his effort.

She may not put all she feels into words in her mind, but in her heart a mother knows this child has said something special to her. He has taken time out from discovering the world to think of her and share the wonder of it. Few, if any, words usually accompany such a gesture, yet the meaning is not missed.

Husbands, too, show their caring in many ways that can be missed if we are looking for something else. Men care about tires on the car because they are concerned about the safety of the family.

When we first got married, I resented it when Don would wait up for me to return from a meeting or playing bridge. I realize now that he wanted to be sure I was safely home before he went to bed.

I'll never forget the woman who helped me to see this. We worked together, and she was divorced. I was complaining to her one day because Don had waited up for me after my bridge group the night before. She said, "Diane, do you know how much I would give to have someone at home who cared enough to wait up for me?" I was taken off guard. I had totally missed the loving message behind what Don was doing.

This isn't something I have learned overnight. But part of the continuing joy I feel in my marriage comes from having learned this skill of listening with my heart.

As a woman begins to develop this quality, it has a profound effect on her marriage. She begins to cultivate a deeper respect for her husband, and he, in turn, begins to respect himself more. With this greater self-esteem comes a new confidence that begins to well up inside him. Feeling sure of his wife's deep respect for him can give a man the confidence to express those words that had seemed so foolish and impossible for him to say before. The rarity of his words makes them all the more precious.

Over the years I have noticed that many of the men who are good at saying just the right thing have become that way with practice. They know how to tell you just what you want to hear because *they have said those same words to many other women.*

Before I was married, I knew a young man like that. Oh, the beautiful things he said to me! He even wrote a poem for me. Later, I found out he had stolen it from the famous poet, Shelley. He surely turned my head—and the heads of a few hundred other women!

When he married, this man became an adulterer. His beautiful words were empty and meaningless. I would rather have a few halting words from a sincere heart than a thousand words from a flatterer.

Unspoken Love

My grandfather and grandmother provided wonderful marriage role models for me. Their home was always a place of warmth and safety.

As a child, I loved my grandfather more than I can express. He had three granddaughters, and I was always sure I was his favorite. Years after my grandfather had passed away, we three adult granddaughters were sitting in a kitchen discussing him. We all adored him, but the interesting thing we discovered was that each granddaughter had grown up believing she alone was his favorite.

How did our grandfather manage to impart such special love to each of his three separate granddaughters, who each lived secure in the knowledge that she was his favorite? Did he spend time telling us how wonderful he thought we were? Did he tell us how beautiful or how clever he thought we were?

This special man was as shy a man as you could find. He finished only the eighth grade in school and never wrote any of us a letter in his life. I can never remember any long heart-to-heart talks or profound wisdom that he imparted to us. Yet I learned a great deal about love from him. There was a special joy in just being with him. I didn't even mind his "scoldings" because it was obvious his heart was not in them.

When I was about nine or ten, my grandfather took me fishing and tried to teach me to fly cast out of a small motor boat. We would get up close to shore in a shallow area, and I would throw out the line several times before getting it stuck in the grass on the shore. My grandfather would just get comfortably settled when he would notice my predicament.

To this day, I can hear him saying, "Oh, ———, Diane, you've gotten it tangled up again!" I would burst out in rapturous giggles, delighted at the expletive that had slipped out. He would pull the boat over, carefully wade to shore, set my line free, and the process would begin again.

My grandfather always loved me just the way I was, and somehow that helped to shape and mold the best parts of my character.

I can never remember a time that he wasn't glad to see me, yet he rarely said it. It was in his face when I came in the room. No wonder each of us granddaughters loved him so much. No wonder each of us was made to feel special. Our relationship with him was built on "heart talk," and words could not replace what his actions said to us.

My grandmother, whom I also adored, was almost totally deaf. The verbal communication between her and my grandfather was extremely limited since neither of them used sign language or had access to modern techniques for the deaf. When they celebrated their fiftieth wedding anniversary, they were as loving and committed a couple as I have ever known.

Philippians 4:8 in the *Amplified Bible* reads, *"If there is any virtue and excellence, if there is anything worthy of praise, think on and weigh and take account of these things [fix your minds on them]."* That Scripture tells us to look beyond the obvious. Consider what some of your husband's everyday actions might be trying to tell you. I think you will be delighted and thrilled by what you find.

A Heart He Can Trust

*A*t the very center of the heart is its tender, precious motivation. In marriage, the importance of this innermost intention can hardly be overstressed. Scripture gives us a beautiful example in Proverbs 31 of the intentions of a virtuous woman's heart.

> *Who can find a virtuous woman? for her price is far above rubies. The heart of her husband doth safely trust in her, so that he shall have no need of spoil. She will do him good and not evil all the days of her life.*
>
> (vv. 10–12)

The *primary motivation* of the virtuous woman was to do good to her husband. Our pastor has said that when he and his wife married, he knew the desire of her heart was to *"do him good and not evil all the days of her life."* You can sense that same attitude in our pastor's wife even today.

A man can sense what is in a woman's heart. When he finds that his heart can safely trust in her, she becomes more valuable to him than rubies.

Contrast this *"virtuous woman"* to the *"strange woman"* mentioned in Proverbs 5:3. Her choices are leading her to hell, and a warning is given to stay away from her *"lest you ponder her path of life; her ways are unstable; you do not know them"* (v. 6 NKJV).

One woman had a heart her husband could safely trust. The other's ways were unpredictable. Her husband never knew how she was going to react. The innermost intention of her heart was not consistent, steadfast, and sure, so he had to hold back a precious part of himself. He held back the part that a woman treasures most: the tender, transparent, vulnerable part. She will never see it because his heart cannot safely trust in her.

For a man's heart to safely trust in his wife, he must know that her response to him will not be based on his own faultless performance. To *trust* means to have a confident expectation. Since life can bring many unexpected circumstances, this trust can be built only on a husband's confidence in the intention of his wife's heart.

Jesus admonished us to *"be ye therefore perfect, even as your Father which is in heaven is perfect"* (Matthew 5:48). I believe He was speaking of this attitude—this innermost intention—of our hearts. We will never walk perfectly before our fellowman, but we can come to the place where the overall intention of our hearts is to please God. I can fall flat on my face before the world, but when the intention of my heart is right, I don't lose my confidence or my joy.

When the intention of my heart is not right, nothing satisfies. Proverbs 23:5 says, *"Wilt thou set thine eyes upon that which is not? for riches certainly make themselves wings; they fly away as an eagle toward heaven."* When I set my eyes on a certain response from my husband, it usually eludes me because I am looking for satisfaction in the wrong place.

The one firm foundation for the intentions of your heart with regard to your husband is this: *"Whatsoever ye do, do it heartily, as unto the Lord, and not unto men"* (Colossians 3:23).

It would be difficult to overstate the value of doing things *"heartily, as unto the Lord."* This brings about positive change in all relationships, especially in marriage. I love God's Word and have confidence in it because I have seen first-hand what it can do in my life. It is powerful, it is wonderful, and it is life-changing!

Heartily as unto the Lord

A friend told me about a woman who had received many complaints from her husband about the way she kept the house—*didn't keep the house* would be more accurate. One day, she decided to turn over a new leaf and began to make an effort to keep the house neat. After years of hearing him complain, she now looked to her husband for words of appreciation for the good job she was doing.

She set her eyes on his reaction. When his response did not measure up to her expectations—and it never will—she became discouraged and shortly gave up her new housekeeping efforts. Notice that her original actions were right, but her intentions were wrong.

If the intention of her heart had been to do it *"heartily as unto the Lord,"* things might have been different. To do something *heartily* means to do it sincerely or genuinely—to do it without restraint. In other words, it means that you are genuinely, sincerely, with all your heart doing it as unto the Lord.

If the woman who made an effort to keep her house neat had been looking to the Lord for her reward and not her husband, she would not have been disappointed. Her husband might have complimented her (as he should), or he might not have. But her joy would have been in doing it as unto the Lord. Then her "new leaf" would have become a positive pattern in her life.

At some point, her husband would probably have noticed the lasting change and would have commented accordingly. Maybe he was waiting to make sure this "new leaf" did not wither on the vine like others she had turned over. In any case, her response to him should not be based on his faultless performance.

As I put this powerful principle from the Word of God into effect in my life, I saw a positive change in my marriage. The intention of my heart changed, and my marriage changed. In many instances, my actions were not that different, but my motivation was. I began to purpose to do my husband good and to look only to the Lord for my reward.

This decision was not just a flash of emotion. It was a lasting change in my innermost heart, and at some point, Don picked this up. Without his conscious knowledge, his heart began to trust in me. He began to open up to me more and more. At the same time, my heart also changed, and he became more pleasing to me. I found greater satisfaction in my marriage than I had ever known before. It was a quiet, progressive change, but it was wonderful.

Deciding to Do Him Good

Living out this commitment to *"do him good and not evil all the days of* [his] *life"* is not always easy. It requires determination to do everything as unto the Lord, but it is worth it.

Not long ago, Don was away for several days on an important business trip. On the day he returned, I planned a happy reunion for him. The minute Don walked in the door, however, I could tell he was absolutely exhausted, physically and mentally. To top it off, he hadn't stopped to eat, so he was also very hungry.

When a man is very tired and very hungry, he is also likely to be *very grouchy!* Don was cross with me, and he was irritable with the kids. It was a far cry from the happy reunion I had planned. My flesh wanted to give him a piece of my mind. How dare he treat us like that! But my spirit wanted to *"do him good and not evil."* I made a conscious choice to follow my spirit. At that moment of decision, things began to change.

I fed him and rubbed his tired back. I ministered to him in every way I knew how. A genuine love began to rise up in me as I ministered to him as unto the Lord. His irritability left, and he began to open his heart to me. Don told me about his day and all he had been through. How glad I was that I had listened to my spirit and not my flesh.

That evening was one of the most special times that we had had in a quite a while. Don couldn't get close enough to me, and later in the week he sent me flowers. What could have been a miserable evening was transformed by the Lord.

Actions without love create martyrs. Marital martyrs reek with self-pity and holy piety, driving away their loved ones with their complaints of continual suffering. This kind of attitude results in bottled-up hostility. There is a vast difference between "taking it" and "giving as unto the Lord."

Jesus beautifully expressed this difference when speaking of giving His own life on the cross. *"No man taketh it from me, but I lay it down of myself. I have power to lay it down, and I have power to take it again"* (John 10:18).

When you give as unto the Lord, you are not operating out of weakness, but from the strength of the very nature of God Himself.

This God-kind of giving brings joy to the giver, as well as to the one who receives it. On the other hand, "giving in" brings resentment and loss of respect to both the giver and the recipient.

God Promises a Reward

Jesus said that when we return good, we have a reward. *"If ye love them which love you* [if you love your husband only when he is lovable], *what reward have ye? do not even the publicans the same?"* (Matthew 5:46).

Jesus often stated that what we do in secret is seen by God and that He rewards us for it openly. *"When thou doest alms...thy Father which seeth in secret himself shall reward thee openly"* (Matthew 6:3–4). We are told to pray *"in secret"* and fast *"in secret"* and God will reward us openly. When I have given my best to God in faith, I excitedly watch, expecting God to do what He said He would do.

When we moved to St. Louis a number of years ago, I saw this truth from God's Word work in a powerful way. I had just recently learned this exciting principle of giving as unto the Lord and looking only to Him for the reward.

We had moved into a large apartment complex, and I couldn't wait to try out this new principle. Much of my conscious time was spent seeking ways to sow to God in secret. I went out of my way to do good, but always as unto the Lord. I never looked to the person involved to return the good or reward me.

48

A wonderful spirit of love began to break out like an epidemic in the complex. People began to comment, "This place was never like this before you came!" The neighbors started caring about each other, and God gave me some of the best and most lasting friendships I have ever known.

With scarcely a spoken word of witnessing, we saw person after person come to know and love the Lord. Entire families were brought into the kingdom of God.

When we started a children's association to raise money for new playground equipment, it was so successful that the *St. Louis Globe-Democrat* ran a front page article on it.

If this intention to *"do good and not evil,"* *"heartily as unto the Lord and not unto man,"* could transform an entire apartment complex, imagine what it can do in your marriage.

In Proverbs 14:22, we are told, *"Mercy and truth shall be to them that devise good."* To *devise* means to work out or create something by thinking. How long has it been since your heart *devised* good for your husband? It will bring mercy and truth and trust into your marriage.

Irreconcilable 4 Differences

*W*henever I hear of a couple getting a divorce and citing "irreconcilable differences" as the reason, I am somewhat amused. At any given time during our twenty years of marriage, Don and I have had at least three areas of irreconcilable differences. Sometimes more than three—sometimes less. The truth is that every married couple—no matter how solid their marriage is—has problem areas that seem to be irreconcilable.

While I am amused when I hear "irreconcilable differences" given as grounds for divorce, I am not amused at irreconcilable differences themselves. They are tough and can be extremely painful. If we don't understand them, they can cause despair and unbearable tension in a marriage.

Irreconcilable differences hurt deeply because they concern areas that cannot be talked out. That's what makes them irreconcilable. They are incapable of being brought into harmony or adjustment. In fact, the more the couple talks about them, the worse the problems become.

Irreconcilable differences are often like sores. When a part of your body is injured, you know it is going to hurt every time you touch it. Yet, at the same time, you can't leave it alone. Some of the most hurtful times in my marriage have been when I have taken it upon myself to try one more time to reconcile the irreconcilable.

This is not to say that these areas will never change. Thank the Lord, they can change! But it takes the power of God and His Holy Spirit to change them. Our fleshly attempts at reconciliation are usually fruitless and can cause added injury or the postponement of healing.

When you sprain a joint, it needs to be put into a cast or another type of restraint to protect it while healing occurs. Problem areas in relationships also require restraint and sometimes need to be left alone for a while. When you stop trying to work things out yourself, the Lord is able to move in and work from the inside.

A good friend of mine shared an interesting situation along these lines recently. She is a lovely woman, yet she has difficulty getting along with her domineering mother-in-law. They have a number of irreconcilable differences. Her mother-in-law's visits to their home, despite her best efforts, would often end in hurtful conflict. Many times through the years they had tried to talk things out, but they had always ended up at the same dead end. In the process, the relationship was badly battered and bruised.

The last time her mother-in-law visited, my friend took a radically different approach. Rather than spending time sitting around the table and visiting over coffee, my friend planned lots of activities. They saw the sights, shopped, and had other relatives over for dinner and games. The mother-in-law has a delightful sense of humor and is ready to try anything. When she left, my friend could honestly say for the first time that she enjoyed having her husband's mother visit.

They had put their irreconcilable differences in a spiritual cast. Perhaps you are thinking, "But isn't that dishonest?" Absolutely not. The Bible tells us to *"avoid foolish and ignorant disputes, knowing that they generate strife"* (2 Timothy 2:23 NKJV). No person has ever been won over by arguing. *Foolish* means lacking forethought or caution.

Where Angels Fear to Tread

An uncle, whom I like very much, visited us one Christmas. We have many things in common, but we also have some serious areas of disagreement. I will never change my mind about these issues, and he will never change his.

That in itself should have caused me to proceed with forethought and caution, but as the saying goes, "Fools rush in where angels fear to tread." I did not accept the sound advice of Scripture to *"avoid foolish and ignorant disputes."* Instead, I thought, "If I just explain how I feel about that one more time, he will see things my way."

Of course, that is not what happened. We got into a heated discussion that did not change him or me one iota! It did, however, put our relationship under a strain for the rest of the visit.

This same principle applies in marriage. All marriages have areas of disagreement that seemingly can't be talked out or worked out in a way agreeable to both parties. This doesn't mean they can never change. God can change anything! But I'm talking about living in harmony with these irreconcilable differences in the meantime. I can tell you right now, "the meantime" is going to seem very *mean* indeed! It will never be soon enough for you. Sometimes it will seem as if you are going to explode if these areas don't change.

Recently, this happened to me. I made the same decision I had made many times before: "If I just explain my position to Don one more time, he will be won over to my way of thinking."

As I was walking over to the sofa to talk to him, I knew in my heart I was making a mistake. But I was overcome with impatience. I just didn't think I could wait another minute. It had to change and change now.

It didn't matter that I had lived with this aggravation for the last ten years, seven months, twenty days, eighteen hours, and thirty-six minutes. I pushed aside the reminder that for the first time I could see God beginning to move in the situation. I wanted immediate progress, and I wanted it *right now!*

Earlier, I had wisely decided to leave this issue in the Lord's hands. Now, I foolishly decided that the Lord was taking too long. It was time for me to help Him out a bit.

These were my thoughts as I approached my dear, unsuspecting mate. On the surface, I came under the guise of "wanting to talk." I knew I shouldn't do it. Even as I write this, I can recall the feeling deep down inside to back off and leave it in God's hands. I had a strong check in my spirit not to do it, but I proceeded anyway.

I had hardly completed the first sentence of my "meaningful dialogue" when I saw Don's face tighten up. The wall God was finally beginning to penetrate became fortified even more. The "meaningful dialogue" became the "predictable dialogue" as the exchange of words became exactly what it had always become: an irreconcilable difference.

If I had left this matter in the hands of the Lord, things would have worked out much better. The saddest part of this story is that *I know* what to do with irreconcilable differences.

Because of our strong personalities, Don and I sometimes clash head-on. But we have learned to separate and pray—then pray and pray some more.

After praying about the situation, I have seen God resolve our differences—sometimes in a matter of minutes. Then, we have come back together, unable to continue the combat. Our hearts have been changed by the power of the Holy Spirit. It is wonderful when reconciliation is so immediate and effective.

But it doesn't always happen so quickly. *Love is patient because God demands it of us.* In Hebrews 6:12 we are told that it is *"through faith and patience* [that we] *inherit the promises."* I have inherited too many promises in my marriage to doubt this powerful Scripture. But the patience part is hard to practice, especially on a regular basis.

The Desires of Your Heart

The Bible says that God will give you the desires of your heart when you delight yourself in Him. (See Psalm 37:4.) I saw the Lord do this for me in two special ways in our marriage.

When Don and I married, two things were particularly disappointing to me. These were areas that in the natural seemed irreconcilable. They were not grave areas of conflict but points of difference that disappointed me.

The first had to do with music. I love classical music. In fact, I like most music, except one—country and western. Don, on the other hand, hated classical music and loved country and western. After our marriage, I found out that Don was tone-deaf, and the only music he could enjoy had to have a strong beat. His preference of music was a far cry from the subtle nuances of violins and flutes. Although this was not a big deal, God knew the disappointment I felt over our not being able to enjoy sharing the same kind of music.

The second area had to do with humor. I came from a large family, and we laughed together a lot. As children, my older brother and I could sometimes get so tickled over just a knowing sideways glance that we would have to leave the church service. Our Irish blood made practical jokes commonplace in our family. They continued to bring delight for years after, and I can recall many happy hours reminiscing about these humorous experiences.

Although Don and I were engaged for almost a year and had dated for a long time before that, in the dailiness of marriage, I found that there were many areas of humor we couldn't share. He had a sense of humor, but it wasn't there when it was needed most. I didn't think he was very funny, and he didn't I think I was either. Worst of all, when I would share some of my precious childhood treasures with him, they often fell flat, robbing me of the joy of them. How I missed being able to laugh and giggle with him as I had with my brother.

I did not tell Don about these two areas of disappointment. I never mentioned how I felt, especially after I found out he was tone-deaf. In fact, I never mentioned them to anyone, but God knew.

As I began to look more and more to God in my marriage, something amazing happened.

The Father gave me little gifts to let me know He had seen my heart and that He could do anything in a marriage.

To fully appreciate what God did, I should tell you that we had been married for over six years when these changes occurred. They weren't just normal, marital adjustments.

One day I was driving Don's car and decided some music would be nice, so I switched on the radio. When I heard violins, violas, symbols, and drums, I could hardly believe my ears. His radio was tuned in to a classical station! I pressed another key, and a similar station was playing a lovely concerto. I'll never forget that day.

When I got home, I mentioned it to Don. He calmly replied, "Yeah, it's funny. I have really developed a taste for classical music." Not only had he developed a taste for it, but he also seemed to have an intuitive understanding of it!

When he began to listen to Beethoven's *Fifth Symphony* (a pastoral symphony), he commented on how he could almost visualize the countryside. Beethoven himself had had to explain this to his musical contemporaries, yet it seemed obvious to Don. Although Don never knew how I had felt about his preference for music, God knew. He supernaturally changed Don without any assistance or nagging from me.

Something else unusual happened about this same time. One day I realized we were laughing together—the good kind of healthy, belly laugh that *"doeth good like a medicine"* (Proverbs 17:22).

After all those years, Don began to delight in my humor. Remarks that had fallen flat before, he now enjoyed immensely. On the other hand, Don had always taken great pleasure in the corniest puns imaginable. Now, all of a sudden, I was enjoying them, too. This great, serious fortress of a man actually learned how to giggle, and you would never persuade our daughters that their dad hasn't always been a great joker.

I'm convinced there are no irreconcilable differences in God, even though sometimes, it seems hard to wait. But, oh, it is worth it!

We're in This 5 for Life

*B*illy Graham and his wife, Ruth, have been married for over forty years. Among her many attributes, Ruth must have a delicious sense of humor. I recall with glee her answer to an interviewer a number of years ago. He asked, "Have you ever considered divorce?"

With scarcely any hesitation, Ruth replied, "Murder, yes; divorce, no!"

This humorous remark revealed something very important about their marriage. As far as the Grahams are concerned, they are in it for life.

I recently read an article by a marriage counselor who made an interesting discovery about commitment in marriage. He said, "Commitment has its own magic." When people finally say yes to their marriage and stop holding a part of themselves in reserve just in case something better comes along, their partner's attitude and their marriage suddenly and dramatically improve.

Many men and women waste precious years wondering, "Did I marry the right person?" If they have serious disagreements or their mates disappoint them, there is always the feeling that life would have been different if they had married someone else.

I came very close to marrying another man. During my first year of college, we were quite serious. We had many things in common. He thought I was wonderful, and I thought he was wonderful.

But God had someone better in mind for me. When Don and I married, we had every kind of adjustment you can have in marriage. If I had married the first man, we probably wouldn't have had as many things to work out. Our first years might not have been as difficult, but our last years could never have been as satisfying.

Opportunities for Growth

Being married to Don has forced me to grow. Many areas that I considered serious problems were actually opportunities for personal growth.

Let me give you an example. I came from a family where sick people were pampered. I mean pampered! My parents raised us in an atmosphere of love and concern—especially when we had any kind of ailment. When Don and I first got married, I thought nothing of staying in bed all day if I wasn't feeling well.

Contrary to my upbringing, Don was raised in a tough, masculine environment. In addition, a good part of his childhood had been spent in anxious concern for his beloved mother who eventually died after a long, devastating illness. By the time we married, the deck was stacked against me. Don had dealt so much with real illness that he had little patience left over for his malingering wife.

On the other hand, for me hospitals and sickness were a backdrop for drama. I had watched enough *Marcus Welby, M.D.,* on TV to know that serious ailments could come on suddenly and with few serious symptoms. My parents had always seemed to understand this.

Don and I, it seemed, were on a collision course. He showed no sympathy and little concern when I wasn't feeling well. "How could I have married someone so uncaring?" I cried angrily. I was sure I must have married the wrong man.

We had a serious problem that provided an opportunity for major growth on my part. Today

I enjoy excellent health and have even become somewhat of a "trooper." I wouldn't dream of wasting a day in bed unless I was truly ill. It has been a very positive growth experience for me to be married to a husband who hates sickness and fights against it with great vigor.

One of the things that has allowed this type of growth on *both* our parts is *commitment.* I was raised in a Catholic background. My thoughts during our first few years of marriage were similar to Ruth Graham's comment, "Murder, yes; divorce, no." One thing Catholics get straight about marriage is that it is for life. That commitment kept us together when nothing else would have. Growing is not easy. Sometimes it is painful, but it is always worth the effort.

In the last twenty years, we have had many opportunities for growth—some of them more serious than others. My heart goes out to young couples who are just beginning their lives together. I know that some of the marriages with the greatest potential for growth are going to have some of the most painful adjustments. I wish I could be their own personal cheerleader. I'd say, "Hang in there! Don't give up. It's going to be worth it."

When I see marriages break up, I am devastated by the lost potential. Some people are never going to become all God intended if they step out of the marital proving ground. Many marriages could be saved if they were based on an ironclad commitment to the vows they made on their wedding day.

The Key Ingredient

Making a marriage work is not just being able to hang on. The rewards come from making it to the rich years that lie ahead when you have worked things out together. Ruth Peale, wife of the late Dr. Norman Vincent Peale, put it this way in her book, *Secrets of Staying in Love:*

"We're one integrated, mutually responsive, mutually supportive organism—and this is such a marvelous and joyous thing that nothing else in life can even approach it. It's the greatest of all adventures."

Mrs. Peale made this remark while speaking to a group of college students at a large Eastern university. They put her on the firing line, but she had plenty of ammunition gained from a lifetime of experience. The question was asked, "If marriage is all that great, Mrs. Peale, why is it that so many marriages end up on the rocks?" She was also asked, "Why can't a man/woman relationship be just as meaningful outside of marriage as in it?"

Her reply was, "Because, it doesn't have the key ingredients. It doesn't have the commitment.

It doesn't have the permanence. It can never achieve the depth that comes from total sharing, from working together toward common goals year after year, from knowing that you're playing the game for keeps. Do you think my husband and I have achieved the relationship we have by just thinking happy thoughts or waving a wand? Don't be absurd! We fought for this relationship! We hammered it out on the anvil of joy and sorrow, of pain and problems, yes, at times, of discouragement and disagreement."

I'm so glad they didn't give up. Think how many lives they have touched and how much good they have produced in this world.

I'm with You for Life

Commitment to marriage also involves being committed to your mate. Don knows with certainty that, next to God, he is the most important person in my life. This has a special effect on a man.

A number of times recently, Don has been in a position to learn about some difficulties other men are going through. He told me about one man who was close to having a nervous breakdown. He was making foolish mistakes on his job and lashing out at those around him. This man was under tremendous pressure and knew he was near the breaking point.

Another man Don knows was experiencing financial trouble. The strain had been great, and he was feeling the weight of it. The sad thing is that neither of these men shared his problem with his wife. Neither felt he could turn to his wife in time of trouble.

When Don told me this, I had difficulty understanding it. I asked him, "Why? Why can't they share the load with the one who would care the most?"

"Because," he said, "they don't feel they can risk opening up to them. They are afraid of what their wives would say." These women may not have expressed it in so many words, but their husbands know that a strong commitment to them is missing—a commitment that would not waver or point a finger even during serious financial loss or emotional strain.

Not long ago Don had a terrible day at work. Everything was going wrong. He was under a lot of pressure, and he called to ask if I wanted to go out for lunch. I had no idea that he was having such a hard day, but I have learned that it is important to make myself available to him. When I adapt to his needs, I am telling Don he is very important and valuable to me.

As he shared with me some of what had happened that day, I could see some of the tension ease. Then he said something precious, "You're a good listener." Actually, I'm not such a great listener, but he knows that he has my undivided attention. He knows that I am committed to him and that what affects him also affects me. He knows that I am his prayer partner in any situation and that I am on his side. He knows that I am committed to him for life.

I have that same confidence in Don. I never wonder where I stand with him; he is always there when I need him. His commitment to me and our daughters is never in question. What a wonderful thing! It is much deeper than romantic love. Commitment says something about the character of the person, and that gives each of us a deep confidence in our relationship.

Covering a Transgression

Have you ever done something really dumb that you instantly regretted? Have you ever said something you wish you hadn't said, then later learned that someone covered your mistake? Someone cared enough about you to choose not to repeat the matter. What a wonderful feeling!

The Bible says, *"He that covereth a transgression seeketh love; but he that repeateth a matter separateth very friends"* (Proverbs 17:9).

It can be devastating to find out that someone has repeated your indiscretion or that someone has been quick to expose your human frailty. It does separate friends, and it can destroy your husband's confidence and trust in your commitment to him.

We had an incident at our church that illustrates this principle well. A woman created a big scene and called those of us involved liars. Her accusations were absolutely false, but no one could convince her otherwise. She actually left the church over the matter.

This incident would have made juicy gossip since it made us look good and her look bad. The church staff, however, chose to cover her transgression in love. No one repeated the matter, and it wasn't brought up as a "prayer request." Even the pastors did not discuss it among themselves. It was covered in love.

What was the end result? About four months later, this woman realized her error and called to apologize. She wanted to be restored to fellowship. It was possible for her to be restored to the church body as a direct result of the church leadership's decision to cover her transgression in love. Even though this loving act was done in secret, I believe her spirit picked it up. This allowed her to admit she was wrong and come back without embarrassment.

This same principle works powerfully in marriage. When your mate knows you will choose to cover his transgressions in love, a strong confidence is established. He can rest assured that you will not expose his mistakes and shortcomings to the world. This builds love, trust, and confidence while promoting healing and openness in your relationship.

Know Your Man

In closing, let me quote Ruth Peale one more time. Her advice is, "Study your man. Study him as if he were some rare, strange, and fascinating animal, which he is. Study him constantly because he will be constantly changing. Study his likes and dislikes, his strengths and weaknesses. Know what makes him happy or angry. Know when he needs encouragement." In other words, show him by your actions that you are committed to him for life.

Make time for him. He'll make time for you. Don't take him for granted, and he won't take you for granted. Encourage him in every way you can. He'll learn to encourage you in ways you never dreamed possible.

Ruth Peale also said, "In this whole area of human relations, women are smarter than men." This wasn't meant as a put-down in any way. Instead, it points to one of the differences between men and women. Proverbs 14:1 says, *"Every wise woman buildeth her house: but the foolish plucketh it down with her hands."* There are areas in a marriage where the woman has an edge, where she sets the standard.

Take the time to become wise about what your husband needs, and you will build your house. Develop a heart he can trust by exhibiting a commitment so real he can feel it and so strong he will feel safe opening up to you. He will share his innermost thoughts and feelings with you, revealing that precious emotional honesty that women treasure so much.

The Change Agent

6

No woman would dream of placing her finest linen tablecloth on a dirty table. No amount of finery would make it seem right. Yet I find people trying to cover over unforgiveness in their marriage by burying it under an outward facade of pleasantries.

Unforgiveness is the cholesterol of the proverbial heart. It's like a clot in a vital artery that slows blood flow to a trickle. Unforgiveness can do the same to love in a marriage.

Our pastor recently said that one of the greatest problems Christians have today is unforgiveness. I have found this to be true. Even when we manage to forgive others, we often have difficulty forgiving ourselves.

Unforgiveness is often hidden under other words or phrases that sound more acceptable.

For instance, we say, "I'm not angry; I'm just hurt." Lingering emotional "hurt" has its root in unforgiveness.

People who would never dream of living for months in unforgiveness can carry hurt feelings with scarcely a thought. This hurt is part of the torment of unforgiveness. Jesus said that we would be delivered to the tormentors if we, from our hearts, do *"not forgive* [our] *brother his trespasses"* (Matthew 18:35 NKJV). You will suffer torment in your marriage if you do not forgive your husband from your heart.

After teaching this principle at a Women's Aglow meeting last year, I talked with a woman who had been hurt by some people in her church. She had carried this hurt for a number of months and seemed powerless to get over it. Now, she realized for the first time that she was really dealing with unforgiveness. By recognizing the source of her hurt, she was able to get over it and free herself from the torment.

Another key to hidden unforgiveness is the phrase, "I can forgive, but I can't forget." I've even heard forgiveness attempted on the basis of divine retribution. "I'll forgive him because God is going to punish him." The Bible does say, *"Vengeance is mine; I will repay, saith the Lord"* (Romans 12:19). But we are warned not to rejoice *"when* [our] *enemy falleth, and let not* [our] *heart be glad when he stumbleth: lest the* LORD *see it, and it displease him, and he turn away his wrath from him"* (Proverbs 24:17–18).

One of the most common ways people approach forgiveness is with rationalizations. They excuse what was done to them by trying to make the wrong more acceptable or worthy of their forgiveness. Proverbs 17:15 says, *"He that justifieth the wicked, and he that condemneth the just, even they both are abomination to the* LORD.*"*

Sin must be either rationalized—made acceptable to our minds—or repented of to be endured. The world is filled with rationalizations that have brought greater and greater sin. Violent crime has increased tremendously as experts have sought to rationalize it by making the criminal no longer responsible for his actions. We hear it said, "He is just a product of his environment. It was poverty that made him that way." Experts who have espoused this philosophy have been dumbfounded at their inability to rehabilitate these "victims of society." Why? Because rationalization does not bring healing.

If every human act could be explained away by circumstances, upbringing, etc., there would be no need for forgiveness—just explanations. There would be no purpose for the Cross or penalty for sin.

Rationalization seeks to make what is wrong right. It is like saying, "You didn't really owe that debt." Forgiveness says, "You owed that debt, but it is wiped clean." Forgiveness removes any sin; rationalization only covers it over. They are very different, but outwardly they can mimic one another. One is healing; the other is not. Forgiveness leads to freedom from sin; rationalization leads deeper into sin.

There are times in every marriage when forgiveness is required. Our first reaction is usually to give a multitude of reasons and excuses. But I have learned the value of being willing to say, "Honey, I was wrong. Will you forgive me?" Or, "What you did really made me angry, but I want you to know that I have forgiven you." It settles the issue, whereas excuses simply build up to be brought out at another time.

Ministering Forgiveness

Jesus illustrated the need to "minister" forgiveness. He was confronted by a man, who was *"sick of the palsy"* (Matthew 9:2). When Jesus looked into this man's heart, He realized the guilt he was carrying. This sick man needed to know he was forgiven before he could accept the healing that Jesus wanted to give to him. The first thing Jesus did was to minister forgiveness to him. Jesus said to him, *"Son, be of good cheer; thy sins be forgiven thee"* (v. 2).

Sometimes our mates—or we ourselves—carry a great weight of guilt. Just as this man could not accept healing until he was forgiven, there are areas in marriage that can never be healed until we minister forgiveness.

A woman I know had an area of sin in her life that she seemed powerless to overcome. Although we prayed about it often, victory never came. One day as we were talking, the subject of her husband came up. Before my eyes, her face visibly changed. It became contorted with hatred and twisted with bitterness as years of unforgiveness came seething to the surface. *Her victory was being blocked by this unforgiveness.* Her marriage would never be made right until she decided to forgive her husband. The power of God could not be manifested in her life as long as she bound her sins to herself with unforgiveness.

It is frightening to realize the destructive force of unforgiveness. Our Lord tells us,

> *If ye forgive men their trespasses, your heavenly Father will also forgive you: but if ye forgive not men* [including husbands] *their trespasses, neither will your Father forgive your trespasses.* (Matthew 6:14–15)

Jesus explained the consequences of unforgiveness in the parable of the unforgiving servant.

*His lord was wroth, and delivered him
to the tormentors, till he should pay all
that was due unto him. So likewise shall
my heavenly Father do also unto you, if
ye **from your hearts forgive** not every
one his brother their trespasses.*

(Matthew 18:34–35, emphasis added)

"From your hearts forgive," Jesus said. You
can begin forgiveness by giving God your free
will to forgive. By choosing in your heart to forgive and looking to God to complete the work,
forgiveness begins.

A friend and I were recently discussing the
power in being willing to forgive. She had experienced a very hurtful situation with a friend one
day. Later, as she went to bed, she was still angry
and distraught. She had been falsely accused,
and it hurt! Lying in bed that night, she tried
to forgive, but forgiveness just wouldn't come.
Finally, she said, "God, you know in my heart
that I want to forgive. I can't seem to do it, but I
am willing. I give this situation to you."

The next morning when my friend woke up,
the forgiveness had taken place! She rejoiced to
find the uncomfortable knot in her heart gone.
When she saw this woman later in the day,
everything was all right between them. God had
brought the forgiveness to pass when all she did
was give Him her "will" to forgive.

Forgiveness is exhilarating to the forgiver and the "forgivee." Zacchaeus, the wicked and cheating tax collector, was so thrilled to learn he was forgiven that he immediately pledged to restore four times everything he had stolen. (See Luke 19:1–10.) Forgiveness allows change to begin.

David and Bathsheba

One of the most beautiful lessons of the restorative power of forgiveness is the story of David and Bathsheba. David looked upon Bathsheba one evening as she bathed, and he lusted after her. (See 2 Samuel 11:2–4.) Perhaps Bathsheba knew the alluring attraction her body would have for David as he glanced at her from his roof. Sure enough, David sent for her, and their *"lust...conceived* [and brought] *forth sin"* (James 1:15).

When Bathsheba was found to be carrying David's child, David tried to deceive her husband Uriah by bringing him home on leave from the army. God did not allow this sin to be covered up, though, for Uriah would not sleep with his wife while his fellow soldiers were still out in the field of battle.

At last, David ordered Uriah to the front lines of the battle where he would most certainly be killed—and he was. As always, unrepented sin brought forth more sin.

This story reads like a sordid soap opera! What David and Bathsheba had done greatly displeased God. Even after David married her, God referred to Bathsheba as *"the wife of Uriah"* (2 Samuel 12:10). The child, who later died, was called *"the child that Uriah's wife bare unto David"* (v. 15).

How could things ever be made right? The same way that all sin can be made right. David repented, and said, *"I have sinned against the* LORD*"* (v. 13). God put David's sin behind him, and for the first time Bathsheba is referred to as David's wife. (See verse 24.)

I often wondered why God would allow Bathsheba to be the mother of Solomon. If I had been God, I would have chosen one of David's other wives to bare Solomon. But God said,

My thoughts are not your thoughts, neither are your ways my ways, saith the LORD. *For as the heavens are higher than the earth, so are my ways higher than your ways, and my thoughts than your thoughts.*

(Isaiah 55:8)

If God had chosen another wife to be Solomon's mother, we would not have such a beautiful and powerful witness of God's forgiveness. Through the restorative power of God's forgiveness, Bathsheba was able to become a fine mother and wife. Solomon, in writing about himself, said he was his *"father's son, tender and the only one in the sight of* [his] *mother"* (Proverbs 4:3 NKJV).

The night I was born again, I remember having an overwhelming sense of God's forgiveness. To understand you are forgiven is to have the weight of the world lifted from your shoulders.

If forgiveness can do so much for us individually, imagine what it can do in marriage. Jesus said, *"To whom little is forgiven, the same loveth little"* (Luke 7:47). If you have much to forgive, you have much love to gain.

As you pray this prayer, let the Lord show you any hidden resentment you may be holding against your husband.

Heavenly Father,

I ask You to reveal to me through Your Holy Spirit any unforgiveness that may be blocking my marital happiness. Show me specific hurts and situations that I need to release to Your healing touch.

Lord, I give You my will to forgive. I can't do it alone, but I believe that You will bring it to pass in my life as I look to You with all my heart. In Jesus' name, Amen.

A Word Spoken in Due Season

*N*ot long ago, I fell down some stairs in our house and broke a bone just below the elbow. My arm was in a cast for six weeks. That was bad enough, but no one had prepared me for how my arm would look when they took the cast off! As I stared at my lifeless and withered arm, I wondered if it would ever be the same again.

Weeks of physical therapy followed. The first exercises I was given seemed ridiculously simple until I tried to accomplish them. By this time, the novelty of a broken arm had long since passed, and no one was too interested in whether or not this grown woman could lift a two-ounce weight by herself—no one except our eight-year-old daughter, Heather.

When I laboriously lifted my arm onto a pillow, only Heather watched with interest and concern. She would tell me, "Careful now, Mom."

It took all my strength to lift that weight, and even that effort was quite painful. Only Heather cheered me on. "You can do it, Mom!

We laughed together at the absurdity of the effort needed to lift so small a weight. When I finally did, she was thrilled. "You did it, Mom! I'm so proud of you!"

Heather will probably never fully understand how much her encouragement meant to me at that time. I never would have regained full use of my arm without diligently doing those exercises. Whenever I think of my broken arm and my painful physical therapy, I remember my little cheerleader who encouraged me when I needed it most.

Encouragement is something we never forget. The effects of it remain with us for a lifetime. You can probably remember as a child receiving a timely compliment or special word of encouragement from a parent, teacher, or coach.

Husbands need encouragement, too. Often, when a man describes his wife, he puts his love and appreciation for her in terms of the encouragement and support he has received. If we could look into a husband's heart at the treasures he has stored, I am sure we would find gems that have to do with the times his wife has encouraged him. A man has a special feeling for a wife who helps him to become all that God intends him to be.

Proverbs 31, the beautiful chapter about the virtuous woman, says, *"Her husband is known in the gates, when he sitteth among the elders of the land"* (v. 23). Her virtue was reflected in the success of her husband. Her marriage partnership with him had a positive effect on his life.

The virtuous woman was careful how she presented herself physically so she would reflect well on her husband. *"She maketh herself coverings of tapestry; her clothing is silk and purple"* (v. 22). This form of encouragement says, "My husband is worth dressing up for. He is special."

Oral Roberts tells about the time he almost gave up. In his early ministry, as a meeting was coming to a close, there was not enough money to pay the rental on the hall. He felt that if God had truly called him, He would also have provided for the financial needs of the ministry. Oral was ready to quit.

When his wife, Evelyn, heard about the situation, she stood up before the huge crowd at the meeting. With trembling voice and shaking hands, she said that she knew God had called her husband but that Oral was ready to give up. She went on to take up a collection that paid for the rental of the hall. Oral has never forgotten Evelyn's encouragement. Today the call on his life is evident to millions, but at that moment of crisis, it was his wife's encouragement and support that made the difference.

James Dobson, the well-known radio psychologist of *Focus on the Family,* has often commented that his wife Shirley believed in him when no one else did. She believed in him before he believed in himself! Today his abilities are recognized around the world. In the beginning, however, it was her encouragement and support that helped sustain him. He has never forgotten it.

Anyone can find encouragement when he has proven himself to be successful. But what a precious thing to find someone who will encourage you when your attempts may seem foolish. No one is excellent at anything in the beginning.

The Value of Encouragement

The name Thomas Edison inspires immediate respect for his genius. He received so many awards in his lifetime that he once joked he had to "measure them by the quart." His creativity gave us the electric light bulb, the phonograph, a more practical telephone and typewriter, and the motion picture camera, just to name a few.

What is less well known about the man, however, is the time as a child he tried to hatch chicken eggs by sitting on them! Or the time he talked a friend into taking a triple dose of "Seidlitz Powders," promising that the resulting gas in his stomach would enable him to fly like a helium balloon!

When Edison started school, the teacher told the district school inspector (within young Edison's hearing) that the boy was "addled," meaning stupid. Can you imagine the effect this could have on a child? It must have been a devastating blow to his self-esteem. I believe God's plan for Thomas Edison's life hung in the balance at that moment.

It wasn't an accident that Edison's outstanding intellect was placed in the hands of an exceptional mother. The Scripture tells us that God knows our name from our mother's womb. *"The LORD hath called me from the womb; from the bowels of my mother hath he made mention of my name"* (Isaiah 49:1).

Through Thomas' egg-hatching experience, through his foolish pranks, and through the teacher's devastating appraisal, Edison had the consistent, undaunted encouragement of his mother. I can imagine that washing raw eggs out of a pair of britches by hand would test the patience of any woman. The "Seidlitz Powders" episode seems funny, but imagine facing the mother of the boy who had taken the medicine!

Many mothers would have been distraught to have had such a son, but Mrs. Edison managed to see him through God's eyes. She saw his potential when no one else did. When the teacher thought Thomas was retarded, his mother took him out of school and taught him at home. Every light bulb in our houses today is a testimony to the power and the value of encouragement.

Wilted Potential

Lack of encouragement can have the opposite effect, however, resulting in lost potential. A good example of this happened right in our neighborhood.

We were excited when the couple living next door to us came to know the Lord. Soon the husband wanted to learn to lead worship in our small group, but he had no music background— just a desire to worship God and help lead others in it.

He bought a guitar and began learning some chords. We could often hear him practicing. After a while, he began to lead singing in small groups. Although he was a little self-conscious, it was evident that he had natural talent. His heart was sincere, and he wanted to serve the Lord, but he doesn't lead singing anymore. In fact, he isn't even attending church.

Why? Because when his talent was just beginning to surface, when he was at his most vulnerable stage, his wife told him how foolish he sounded. His singing was an opportunity for her to make a joke and get a laugh. If he brought out his guitar to play and sing for someone, she would grimace or remark with great sarcasm, "Boy, are you in for a treat!"

We will never know the full potential of the talent God placed in this man because it wilted on the vine from lack of encouragement. Today this wife is reaping a bitter harvest.

We can make the foolish assumption that we outgrow our need for encouragement. As adults, it is hard to find people who will reassure, exhort, and impel us to "Go for it!"

A few years ago, I decided to participate in a swim marathon. My goal was to swim two miles in the competition, so I worked hard to build up my distance. I was well into my thirties at this time, and I knew most of the other competitors would be much younger. Every day at practice, when I pulled my weary body out of the water, I hoped someone would notice how far I had swum. Like a child, I looked around expecting someone to say something to encourage me. Occasionally the pool manager would ask me how many laps I had done, and that made my day!

I did swim two miles in the marathon, but I often wondered how far I could have gone with committed encouragement from someone. God has placed talents and abilities in every human being, but many will never be realized unless someone encourages us.

Releasing Potential

In the natural world, we are judged by what we are. God, on the other hand, looks at what we can be. Those two ways of looking at ourselves produce different results in our lives. One binds us to the past and to what we secretly fear we are. The other releases hope, excitement, and freedom to reach for the stars—to reach for all God has for us. Our potential is unlimited in God!

The Bible is full of stories about released potential. Moses, the son of a Hebrew slave, delivered an entire nation out of bondage. David, the shepherd boy, became a king. A young village girl named Mary gave birth to the Savior, and Peter, a Galilean fisherman, became the spiritual leader of the early church in Jerusalem.

Today we can look at men like Oral Roberts, a simple preacher who has taken the healing power of God to his generation. With God's help, he brought millions of people to the Lord and built one of our finest universities.

Ronald Reagan is probably the only leader in the world to have successfully made the transition from actor to powerful world leader.

Both these men have had the strong support and faithful encouragement of their wives. Standing alongside their husbands, these wives have exhorted, impelled, and reassured them with, "You can do it. You and God are a winning combination." These men couldn't have done it without God, but perhaps they wouldn't have done it without the encouragement of their wives.

God takes special pleasure in seeing us live up to our potential. He sees all He put within us and all we can become in Him. When Gideon was hiding from the Midianites, thrashing wheat in a wine press, the angel of the Lord called him a *"mighty man of valour"* (Judges 6:12). To the natural eye, Gideon was anything but a mighty man of valor. He was so scared he was hiding in the wine press.

In fact, Gideon did not see himself as a brave warrior. To paraphrase his reply to God, Gideon said, "Me? You must be kidding! I am nothing; I'm the least in my father's house." But God saw his potential, and Gideon saved Israel from the Midianites. He was a *"mighty man of valour"* after all!

Bringing Out the Best

An important aspect of marriage involves being sensitive to your mate's potential. Through your encouragement, you can help your spouse develop his or her unique talents and abilities. I love the way the book of Proverbs acknowledges this need, *"A word spoken in due season, how good it is!"* (Proverbs 15:23 NKJV).

A word at the right moment can make the difference between success and failure, between talents being brought forth to the glory of God or talents atrophied from lack of use. Encouraging your mate with a kind word can make the difference between a good marriage and a great one.

I have an unmarried friend who is beautiful, intelligent, and talented. She also has a strong faith in God. Since I have known her, she has been believing God for a husband. But she has quite a list! He must be tall, good-looking, financially successful, self-confident, and, of course, he must be a mighty man of God.

Perhaps someday she will find this man. Perhaps they will get married and live happily ever after. They may have a good marriage, but they will never have a great marriage. His love for her will never reach the depth of the man whose wife believed in him, encouraged him, and helped him to become all God intended him to be. My friend will never have the satisfaction of seeing potential reached and knowing in her heart that God allowed her to be a part of that process.

Molded plastic can never have the value or beauty of something that has been carved out of a block of rough oak. Only through time and effort do the excellent grains of the wood begin to show so all can see them. Your encouragement can help to bring out the beauty in your marriage.

The Work of a Man's Hands

The talents your husband uses in his work are often gifts of the Holy Spirit. In Exodus 31:2–5, the Lord said,

> *See, I have called by name Bezaleel....I have filled him with the spirit of God, in wisdom, and in understanding, and in knowledge, and in all manner of workmanship, to devise cunning works, to work in gold, and in silver, and in brass, and in cutting of stones, to set them, and in carving of timber, to work in all manner of workmanship.*

Your husband's skills and abilities are God-given talents that require your respect and interest.

Jesus acknowledged the value of a man's work when He provided a miracle catch of fish for Peter and his fellow fishermen at Gennesaret. (See Luke 5:1–11.)

Proverbs 22:29 says, *"Do you see a man who excels in his work? He will stand before kings"* (NKJV).

Your husband's work may not seem spiritual to you, or perhaps it doesn't seem important to you. But God felt it was important enough to make it a part of the blessing of Abraham. The Lord said He would *"bless all the work of thine hand"* (Deuteronomy 28:12).

If you don't understand this, you can fail to be supportive of your husband's work. Your lack of support and respect for what he does comes out in a hundred ways. If you are resentful when he has to work overtime or disinterested when he discusses situations at work, he can sense how you feel. Do you share his joy at successes and his despair over failures, or aren't they really important to you? You need to realize that God cares about your husband's work because it is part of the total person He created him to be.

I have tremendous respect for the God-given talents and abilities my husband Don uses in his work. Don senses my support for what he does, and it undergirds and helps him. God has given him special abilities in the area of engineering. I have as much respect for what he does as I do for any pastor or teacher because I know that Don's abilities come from God just as theirs do.

Men in the secular work force are usually out there where the action is. They are the *"salt of the earth"* (Matthew 5:13) in the marketplace and a light in the darkness of the business world. Don is a witness in his job, and he is able to touch people who would never go to church. He is a force for righteousness where it is desperately needed, and I have tremendous respect and appreciation for the way God uses him.

Reaping Support

Today Don owns a successful engineering firm. Recently, his firm won an award for engineering achievement from the Society of Professional Engineers.

When Don and I married, however, I had no idea that he had this special ability in engineering, and neither did he! Don's earlier academic experience had been a shambles. In college his grades were so poor that at one point he had to drop out of engineering. When we were first married, he worked in oil field construction. After two years, he decided to go back to school. This time Don made the dean's list! What a change. This time he had someone to encourage him. While he was in school, I became the primary support of the family. Don has never forgotten my encouragement and assistance during those two years.

After a successful career in the engineering field, Don felt it was time to start his own consulting firm. This meant giving up an excellent position with a well-established company and losing the assurance of a monthly paycheck. But I believed in Don and had faith that God was leading us. Don's first office was just a tiny back room in a building with another company. I can still remember our excitement when he got his first project. His smile was as big as all outdoors that evening.

When Don moved into his first suite of offices, I helped him decorate it. We picked out furniture together and selected wall hangings. It's been a joy and honor for me to have a part in his work. When I look at my husband, I know he is a man who is living up to his potential. I see the satisfaction in him, and I benefit from it each day of my life.

When I began to write and teach, pastors commented on how much Don encouraged me in my ministry. One said, "I've never seen a husband so supportive of his wife's ministry. He must not have an insecure bone in his entire body!"

I can't tell you how I feel when I hear Don reply, "You don't know how she has always encouraged and supported me in everything I have done. I figure it's my turn now." It amazes me to think that all it took to reap such love and support was to believe in his potential, to lift him up a little when he was down, and to be interested in what he was interested in. What a blue-chip investment encouragement is!

Letting Him Lead

The more I learn to know God through prayer and the study of His life-changing Word, the more potential I see in Don and in other people. The first word God spoke to my heart in a direct way had to do with Don and his God-given potential. I have never forgotten these words or the impact they have had on our life together.

This happened many years ago, and at the time, my prayers about Don were more like complaints. His faults had not escaped my notice, and I was sure God needed to fully understand Don's inadequacies before He could move in his life. I was most willing to use my prayer time to help God out in this regard.

I had particularly noticed that Don was lacking in the area of spiritual leadership in our home. Although I had been born again and filled with the Spirit a few years before Don was, I knew it was God's plan for the husband to be the spiritual leader of the family.

I had tried leaving meaningful literature in frequented places, but they were left untouched. I offered to read the Bible out loud to Don (since I was reading anyhow), but he wasn't interested. Finally, when all else failed, I prayed, "Lord, Your Word says that the man is to be the spiritual leader in the home, and you know that Don isn't," and so on and so on.

Somewhere around this time, God spoke to me. It took me so off guard that I remember stopping dead in my tracks. My "prayer" had suddenly become a two-way conversation, and it changed my life. What the Lord spoke was a revolutionary idea to me. It wasn't at all what I had expected.

The Lord said, "If you will look to Don as your spiritual leader, I will raise him up to be." God was asking me to do something by faith—not faith in the Don that my natural eyes could see, but faith in the potential God had placed in him.

I had been waiting until Don proved himself as the strong spiritual leader I desired him to be before I looked to him for leadership. It was like waiting for a child to run before you encourage his first steps. God was saying, "He won't get there without your encouragement and faith."

This was a powerful principle, and I have never forgotten it.

Today Don is the spiritual leader of our home, and his counsel and insight have blessed me time and time again. His growth began when I obeyed God and looked at Don with God's eyes, seeing the spiritual potential in him.

Ways to Encourage

Words, written or spoken, are certainly not the only meaningful form of encouragement. In fact, if words are not sincere, they are nothing but empty flattery. Encouragement must come from the heart to be of genuine value.

Sometimes we need God's help to see the abilities He has placed in people around us. Once you have seen the potential in others, how do you help to bring it out? Perhaps you want to be an encourager, but you have received little encouragement yourself. Perhaps you just don't know how to encourage others.

One way to encourage others is to be willing to give of your time and attention. Be willing to listen to ideas while they are still ideas rather than well-thought-out plans. Sometimes a good idea becomes a great idea when someone takes the time to listen.

Sharing with someone else helps bring concepts into reality. An idea can be floating around in your head, but when you share it with a supportive listener, it moves into another category. It is no longer just an idea. It becomes a direction, something you can move toward. When another person sees value in your ideas and plans, they no longer seem foolish or worthless.

Giving your husband quality attention may mean readjusting your schedule at times. I have learned the value of being available to my husband. Sometimes when he invites me to go for a walk, he is really saying, "I have an idea I want to bounce off you." Sometimes when he invites me to lunch, he is really saying, "I have something I want to talk to you about. See what you think of this."

Spending time with your husband is more important than the laundry you feel must get done right now. Being available to him is more important than the book you are in the middle of reading or the TV program you are watching. Be sensitive and learn to adapt, or these precious times of sharing with your husband can be lost forever.

Can you imagine how important it was for Nancy to be willing to listen when Ronald Reagan first shared the secret that had been running through his mind? Her response at that moment probably had a great deal to do with bringing his dream to pass.

Another powerful way to encourage others is through prayer. I can see the effect my prayers have on my husband and his work when I am diligently praying for him. Prayer makes a difference. He may not even know it in the natural, but in the spiritual realm, he is being built up. He can feel it in his inner man.

During a particularly difficult time in our lives, Don would come home from work some days and ask me, "Have you been praying for me?" He could feel the power in his spirit, and it helped him when things were tough.

Every day I pray that he will have wisdom in his work and favor in the marketplace. I ask the Lord to prosper all that Don sets his hand to as God has promised. (See Deuteronomy 28:8.) I also pray for the men who work for Don and for their families. Don feels my support, and it has a powerful effect on his life. My prayers help him to become all that God intends for him to be.

In Due Season

Most people feel somewhat foolish and self-conscious when they try something new. They are usually unsure of themselves. That is when they need *"a word spoken in due season."* What is the *"due season"* spoken of in Proverbs 15:23?

The *"due season"* is *the time of need.* Pats on the back later will never mean what a few words of hope and confidence indicate in the beginning of a new project. In fact, some things will never be learned, some victories will never be won, some successes will never be experienced without encouragement in the *"due season."*

God often gives me special Scripture verses or words to encourage Don. They have more power to encourage than anything I have ever said on my own. God's Word is healthful and life-giving. It expands your vision beyond anything you alone could dare hope.

It is a great tragedy to see this powerful force sometimes used to condemn rather than encourage. Some wives use God's Word not to uplift their husbands but to tear them down.

It used to bother me to hear people in mental hospitals quote from the Bible with great accuracy. God's Word is so precious and has brought such healing to my life that I couldn't understand how someone could have this *"two-edged sword"* (Hebrews 4:12 NKJV) and still be mentally unbalanced. Then I began to notice a consistent pattern in their use of the Word. They always directed the verses at other people in a negative way, quoting the judgment of God without the love of God.

The Bible says, *"In the beginning was the Word, and the Word was with God, and the Word was God"* (John 1:1). God's Word is not just a book of moral guidelines and uplifting stories; it has a supernatural quality. It is powerful! The nature of God Himself is in His Word, and, in ways we cannot fully understand, it must be spoken with love.

You will never experience the joy and confidence that God's Word can bring if you are using His Word against your mate. Use the Word to uplift, to encourage, and to support your husband, and he will learn to love the Bible. If any correction is needed, God will chasten him in a way that will be to his greatest benefit and yours as well.

Do you see your mate's potential? Do you watch for the talents and abilities God has placed in him? Do you encourage your husband to develop these talents? Do you support him in his work? Are you willing to take a chance on him? Does he feel your support way down in his inner being from your prayers and attitudes?

God has worked miracles in our lives as we have encouraged one another in our God-given potentials. Ask God to help you see your mate as He sees him. It will refresh you and give you a new vision for your life together.

Body Ministry 8

At a Christian women's seminar recently, I was asked to address the subject of sex. After saying yes, I began seriously to consider what I should share. Through the years, I had read many books on sexual love in marriage. Although almost all I'd read had been presented from a Christian perspective, very little of this material had been helpful to me.

I decided to share the most significant things I had learned personally from twenty years of marriage. With fear and trepidation, I committed myself to being frank in my teaching, having no idea how it would be received. To my astonishment, what I said hit home with the majority of the women, and the response was overwhelming.

All the next week I received phone calls and letters at my home. The following Sunday at church, the men's reactions were even more remarkable. Total strangers walked up and hugged me. Some commented, but most just smiled. Their reactions touched me deeply.

About two weeks later, I was walking by a construction site when one of the big, burly workers approached me and asked gruffly, "Aren't you Diane Hampton?" I gulped and admitted that I was. "My wife was at that seminar you taught, and I just wanted to thank you. Whatever you told her really helped our marriage." Then he walked away. My heart was deeply moved by his gratitude.

What startling revelation was unveiled at this seminar. What sensuous secret did I share? None. Instead, I believe that their hearts were touched in the real, everyday world in which marriages are built. And when you touch a woman's heart, you touch her marriage.

In the last few generations, woman have been exposed to a wide range of sexual ideas. At one time a puritanical extreme dictated that women were never to enjoy sex. Today women are told by the media that sexual freedom is the norm. Almost daily, we are bombarded with sexual pressures.

In our efforts to present sex as good, we have moved into another extreme that says sex is perfect. The world has the idea that there is some mystical "super sex," which is nothing less than earthshaking. They say experiencing anything less means you've got trouble in your marriage. No wonder people are hesitant to speak frankly about sex!

Reality is more toward the middle ground. Sex can be wonderful, but it isn't always. There are just too many variables, including stress, physical illness, fatigue factors, and what I call "body clocks."

Internal Gauges

It has been valuable for me to understand that bodies run on daily cycles. We all have internal "body clocks." Some people are morning people, for example. They wake up early, and staying up late is like fighting off the effects of a strong sleeping medication.

Other people are night owls. They are just getting their second wind as the sun goes down.

These internal time mechanisms have a tremendous effect on your sexuality. If you are a morning person, your peak of sexual responsiveness might be right after supper. Waiting until eleven o'clock in the evening to make love can be disastrous! Genuine responsiveness at seven o'clock becomes drudgery at eleven o'clock. A night owl, on the other hand, might be just getting in the mood at that time.

When sex happens doesn't matter in the least. Understanding when your spouse is most responsive, though, is very helpful. One of a young mother's greatest threats to sexual fulfillment can be physical fatigue. A woman who has been chasing after a toddler all day, in addition to fixing dinner, driving car pools, cleaning house, and nursing a newborn, is likely to be utterly exhausted by bedtime.

The husband has most likely worked a full day as well. He comes home and is ready for a well-deserved rest. After dinner and perhaps some games with the kids or an evening of TV, he, unlike his wife, may be feeling pretty frisky by bedtime. To his beleaguered wife, his advances are about as welcome as "Jack the Ripper."

Experiencing such frustration a number of times can cause a couple to reach some wrong conclusions. He may feel he is no longer attractive to his wife and that she does not desire him. She wonders what is wrong with her and why her body doesn't respond to her husband's advances.

After I taught this seminar, one young married woman came up afterward to thank me. She said, "I was afraid there was something wrong with me!"

Understanding the Male Response

I am going to try to clarify how a man is not like a woman by explaining how he is like a woman—an ambitious project indeed!

A man is like a woman in that both have hormones that affect them physically and emotionally. A man is not like a woman because his hormonal cycle is very different. A woman's hormonal cycle is basically 28 days; a man's cycle is more like every 48 hours. While a woman's responsiveness gradually rises, peaks, and then gradually declines throughout a month's time, a man's responsiveness can rise, peak, and fall within a day's time. (See graph on page 110.)

From a hormonal aspect, sexual response is going to vary significantly in men and women. On a woman's 28-day cycle with nothing else considered—and there are always other factors to consider—there will be peak days of responsiveness as well as days of minimum responsiveness.

It is helpful to understand this cycle and the effect it has on women sexually. Just as fireworks are easiest to find around the Fourth of July, a woman should know her body well enough to realize when her "Fourth of July" is ready to occur. She should enjoy the fireworks at that time without feeling that every day should be a holiday. We just aren't made that way!

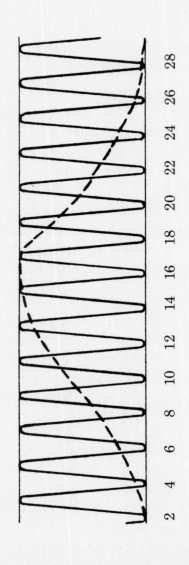

Hormonal Responsiveness—Male versus Female

— = Male Responsiveness   - - - = Female Responsiveness

Of course, this does not mean that a woman will not experience sexual desire at other times. It simply means that her sexual responsiveness from a hormonal aspect will probably rise, peak, and fall during certain days of her 28-day cycle.

A man, on the other hand, has a much more urgent, consistent sexual desire peaking approximately every 48 to 72 hours (every two to three days).

When a man is not able to express his sexuality in marriage, the hormonal response is similar to what a woman experiences in premenstrual tension. He becomes edgy and irritable, and he may feel that he is experiencing unusual stress. Nearly every wife has noticed the difference having sex makes in her husband's disposition.

If a wife doesn't have some understanding of these things, she is likely to think some beastly instinct has possessed her husband. The Bible says that God put this desire in man. (See Genesis 2:24.) The continuation of the human race was riding on it, so God didn't take any chances. He made the sexual drive strong, compelling, and persistent.

As a young bride, this was one of my most difficult sexual adjustments. Growing up in a very open family, I certainly knew the "facts of life." But until you have experienced lovemaking in marriage, you really don't even know what questions to ask.

Afterward, it was just too personal to share. Nothing I had read or heard prepared me for the insatiability of a man's sexual appetite. Part of the adjustment of marriage is coming to grips with your sexuality and his sexuality in day-to-day living.

What I have just shared is intensely personal, and I wouldn't do it without good reason. I would be much more comfortable saying that everything was perfect from the first night and that we never had serious adjustments or misunderstandings. But it isn't true, and hiding the facts won't help anyone. Our situation was not unique at all. In fact, it is probably what occurs in most marriages.

Making Adjustments

We hear a lot of talk about sexual perfection, but I'm convinced we never totally arrive there. Rather, it is a matter of continual adjustment. There are wonderful periods of pleasure followed by more adjustments.

Nothing in life is constant. Why should we believe that this area of our life would be? The best techniques become timeworn in the dailiness of marriage. Our bodies change, and we grow older. We have children and must adjust to the differences they bring to our lifestyles.

Sexual expression can become difficult at certain times in our lives. Overloaded schedules or working the night shift can create changes in our sexual responsiveness. Tragedy or sickness can cause our spirits to plummet and lessen our sexual desire.

Sexuality remains viable in marriage not by arriving at perfection, but by being willing to keep trying for it. We must be willing to keep on working out the differences and adjusting to the changes. The real problems develop when we give up, when we are no longer willing to work at it, or when our hearts become hardened.

Without sexual expression in marriage, something precious, warm, and spiritual is missing. An intangible bonding agent is lost that makes the marriage relationship different from any other relationship. A good, healthy sexual relationship is worth working for and worth pursuing.

Sex is like mastering the piano. You don't stop playing just because you come to a difficult part. In the long run, mastering the difficult parts brings the greatest satisfaction.

God's Secret to Eve

At the beginning of this chapter, I said that only a fraction of what I had learned was actually helpful to me. What I am going to share now was very helpful. It has to do with what Jesus said about *"out of the abundance of the heart"* (Matthew 12:34). I have learned that out of the abundance of the heart, the *body* speaks.

To fully understand this idea, we need to look all the way back to the creation of man and woman. When Adam first saw Eve, his response was immediate. He was ready to leave everything to *"cleave"* to her (Genesis 2:24). God did not have to ask him what he thought of Eve. Nearly every man has the capacity to just look at his Eve and he's ready to cleave!

To the woman, however, God had to give a brief explanation. Try to visualize Him talking to Eve. "Now, Eve, listen to me. Pay attention to what I am saying because this is important. Eve, *'your desire shall be for your husband'"* (Genesis 3:16 NKJV).

God was saying, "Eve, you are to desire, to wish for, to crave, and to want your husband." Why would God take the time to explain this point to her? Because she was created in such a way that unless her mind and heart were involved, unless she learned to desire her husband, the sexual organs in her body would not function properly.

A man cannot possibly satisfy a woman sexually without her involvement in this area. We need to learn to desire our husbands. How? Go to the treasures you've been storing in your heart. Think about them. Learn to think about your husband and what you like about him. The lover in the Song of Solomon practiced this principle.

• *"A bundle of myrrh is my wellbeloved unto me"* (Song 1:13). I love my husband's aftershave!

• *"His legs are as pillars of marble, set upon sockets of fine gold"* (Song 5:15). He is so strong!

• *"Thou art fair, my love;...thou hast doves' eyes"* (Song 1:15). My husband is so handsome!

• *"His mouth is most sweet: yea, he is altogether lovely. This is my beloved"* (Song 5:16). My husband is my friend and lover.

Notice how the maiden singled out certain attributes that she admired about her beloved. She likes his eyes and thinks of them. Many women notice eyes. She likes his hair, so she thinks about it. Many women are attracted by hair—or the lack of it! Baldness is very masculine. Some women find hands and arms very appealing.

I know which of my husband's physical attributes are attractive to me. He is large and impressive in stature, and I am strongly attracted by the physical bulk of him. His hairy chest is also very appealing to me.

Study the physical attributes of your husband. Learn to store up what is attractive to you and think about those details when you think of him.

I deeply admire Don's willingness to care for our family and our needs. In my heart, I have stored memories of all the times he has worked hard to provide for us.

When we first married, Don worked in oil field construction. He was young, strong, and determined to succeed. Often he would come home covered with mud. Sometimes he had been out in the cold or rain all day long, yet he never complained and always willingly provided for my needs.

I admire Don for being his own man. He makes his own decisions and is not influenced by what other people think. This attribute is very attractive to me.

When we first started our family, he knew it was important to me to stay home with our children. In the beginning, this made our finances tight because I had worked until Jennifer was born. Suddenly, we had to get by on one check instead of two. But he never questioned the importance of what I was doing and was never influenced by seeing other wives going back to work.

Today Don owns and manages an engineering firm, but he has never let his priorities get out of order. The girls and I never question where we stand with him. That is exceptional for a man as successful as he is.

Becoming One Flesh

During the day I often dwell on the things I love about Don. By the time he gets home, my heart is overflowing and my body is ready. He walks into an atmosphere charged up with love.

If I don't take time to desire him, to crave him, and to admire him, things are not the same. That is my part of the deal. It is the way God made me. No sexual techniques are ever going to replace this need in a woman.

In such an atmosphere of love, something special develops that I call "body ministry." There is a vast difference between meeting needs and body ministry. As I learned to desire Don and to prepare my heart, I began to experience a new sense of "becoming one flesh."

It is similar to what a mother experiences with her newborn baby. She receives a pleasurable feeling from covering her baby when he is cold. When her baby is crying, she is not comfortable until he is quiet and content. This sense of oneness is so intense that a nursing mother can merely hear her baby crying and milk comes into her breasts.

This relationship between a mother and her child resembles in many ways the oneness that God intended to occur between a husband and a wife.

You can begin to feel in your body what your husband is feeling in his body. When Don is tired, I "feel" his tiredness. When he has worked at a desk all day long, I can sense the tightness in his shoulders. I minister to him by rubbing his back. Sometimes when he has been standing all day, I massage his tired feet.

I experience a pleasurable feeling from meeting these needs. This "becoming one flesh" has added new depth to our relationship. When it began, Don could sense that something was different, and it delighted him. I am sometimes shocked at how insensitive some women can be to the physical needs of their husbands. I have seen men literally sagging with exhaustion and fatigue, yet their wives seem oblivious to it! These women are missing the beautiful oneness that keeps the physical side of their relationship from becoming routine.

As you think up new ways to give pleasure to your husband, a lovely body-to-body communication develops and gives you pleasure at the same time. Learn to desire your husband, to wish for, to crave, and to want him. It can transform your marriage.

Rejoicing

*P*roverbs 5:18 says, *"Rejoice with the wife of thy youth."* Every happy marriage I know has this element of rejoicing—a willingness to pursue godly pleasure together.

Rejoicing plays an important part in marriage. The time spent enjoying one another's company can make the difference between a boring, humdrum relationship and one that is stimulating and healthy.

A lifetime commitment like marriage can get bogged down in the daily drudgery of routine. Couples need change and variety at times, and this fifth chapter of Proverbs tells you what to do: *rejoice.* Rejoicing keeps your love fresh and enthusiastic. Spending quality time together helps you and your husband gain perspective and renew your shared vision.

Earlier this year, Don and I made plans to celebrate our twentieth wedding anniversary. We didn't want to observe it; we wanted to *rejoice* in it. It is wonderful to be "the wife of Don's youth." We have many joys to look back on together and many blessings to look forward to in the future.

Don and I decided to do something special for our anniversary—just the two of us. After many happy hours pouring over various travel brochures, we finally decided to take a trip to Jamaica. We both love the sun and the water.

As the departure date drew closer, our daily schedules grew tighter and tighter. After one particularly frustrating day, I happened to drop by Don's office. The thought of the many detailed preparations for the trip seemed overwhelming. I began to think of other things we could do with the money we were spending—like put down a new kitchen floor. I said to Don, "Everything is getting so complicated! Maybe we should just forget about this trip."

For an instant, a look passed over his face that reached down into my heart. Almost immediately, however, Don regained himself and commented, "Whatever you want to do is all right with me."

Thank God, I had seen the expression on his face! This trip—this time of pleasuring and rejoicing—was more important to him than I had dreamed. I quickly changed my tune, silently thanking God that I had not turned my back or been looking down when Don spoke.

Before I left his office that day, we were again happily making travel plans. God used this experience to reiterate something valuable that I had almost forgotten. This trip was not just some frivolous expenditure; it was an investment in one of our greatest treasures—our marriage.

Don and I came back from Jamaica refreshed and renewed with a thousand precious memories. While we were there, Don and I had long walks and restful times to discuss things I had wanted to talk to him about for months. We had talked at home in a hit-and-miss fashion, but we had not been able to share all that was in our hearts.

It was good to return home with a fresh outlook on situations that faced me daily. In fact, I didn't realize how much I had needed the trip until we got back.

I wonder what effect it has on a marriage to continually put important discussions on the back burner. I know the effect it had on our marriage to have this time of togetherness: it was very positive and unifying.

We rejoiced together, and the experience was beautiful and irreplaceable to us as a couple. I wouldn't have missed it for anything, yet I almost did by setting wrong priorities. For a moment, I forgot that rejoicing is important in a marriage.

God Himself set up feast days or times of celebration and called His people to observe them. (See Exodus 23:14–16.) Celebrations are important to God, and they are essential to a marriage.

To *"rejoice with the wife of thy youth"* is not the same as taking a family vacation. It is important to realize the difference.

In our relationship with God, we need time together with our church family, but we also need time alone with our Lord. In marriage we need family vacations, but we also need time alone with our mates. We need time to renew our goals, share our hearts, and listen to God speak to us together as one unit before Him.

Making Time for Rejoicing

Don and I know a very successful businessman. During his initial stages of success, this man allowed time for rejoicing. He and his wife would often get away for a weekend, and their marriage was filled with joy.

As he became more and more successful, however, this man found less and less time for rejoicing. The years slipped by with no periods of relief, and the joy was less evident in their home. As pressures began to build, this businessman made some foolish mistakes and errors in judgment. His success started to slip away; and the more he felt it leaving, the harder he worked.

For eight years he and his wife did not get away together for a fresh look at their marriage or a new perspective on life. By the end of those eight years, this man had lost almost everything. Instead of increasing his success, he nearly destroyed it. His marriage was damaged, and much of the vitality and joy in their relationship was gone. This husband failed to heed the Scripture to *"rejoice with the wife of thy youth."*

Priorities sometimes get misplaced in a marriage. While husbands are often consumed by their jobs, wives have a tendency to get caught up in church work or community activities. Fellowship with our heavenly Father becomes hurried, and time for rejoicing with our mate gets pushed aside by other responsibilities.

Becoming overly involved in too many areas is a constant problem with me and our lifestyle. Periodically I have to drop out of some activities in order to have fellowship with the Lord and time to spend with Don.

When I first began to have opportunities to speak and teach, I never dreamed of turning down any invitation. Often I was going out three nights a week. My prayers were becoming mechanical repetitions squeezed into an ever busier schedule. It wasn't that I didn't make time for God: I had Him scheduled at the beginning of my day. But there was not enough time to wait on Him and listen to Him speak to me.

God can't be boxed into a certain time period. Listening to Him and learning from His Word require more than a hasty reading from a daily Bible-reading schedule.

In the same way, a healthy marital relationship requires more than a few hurried chats over the morning newspaper or brief phone calls from work. Love needs long, unstructured periods of time for listening, learning, and recommitment.

Faithfully Satisfied

It is no accident that the same chapter of Proverbs dealing with rejoicing also mentions faithfulness. Rejoicing keeps our relationship fresh and helps us to remain faithful to our marriage partner.

The rewards of fidelity in marriage are beautifully affirmed by these wise words of Solomon:

Let thy fountain be blessed: and rejoice with the wife of thy youth. Let her be as the loving hind and pleasant roe; let her breasts satisfy thee at all times; and be thou ravished always with her love.
(Proverbs 5:18–19)

In a relationship based on total trust and fidelity, you can be *"ravished"* with love, and satisfied with your mate.

Most of the fifth chapter of Proverbs deals with the subject of faithfulness in marriage. It warns of the dangers of strange women when it says,

The lips of a strange woman drop as an honeycomb, and her mouth is smoother than oil: but her end is bitter as wormwood, sharp as a twoedged sword. Her feet go down to death; her steps take hold on hell.
(vv. 3–5)

The lure of infidelity has a bitter end. In no uncertain terms, we are instructed to *"drink waters out of thine own cistern, and running waters out of thine own well"* (v. 15).

Restoration and Recreation

Paul made an interesting point in his first letter to the Corinthians when he asked, *"Doth not even nature itself teach you...?"* (1 Corinthians 11:14). Nature does teach us about God.

Jesus often used examples from nature to teach us about Himself and His principles.

David, too, described the renewal that God often brings to us when we take time to rest and appreciate what God has created. He said, *"He maketh me to lie down in green pastures: he leadeth me beside the still waters. He restoreth my soul"* (Psalm 23:2–3). The peacefulness and refreshment of being outdoors can help the process of restoration.

My grandparents, who were healthy and active well into their eighties, had a lifelong habit of sitting outside in the evenings. This practice helped to restore their souls. It gave them time alone together to review the events of the day and reflect on the beauty of God's creation.

It is important to encourage your husband to find time to be outside where he can relax. If, however, you resent the time he spends on sports and hobbies, they become a time of tension and guilt for him instead of a time of restoration. Some of that beautiful quality of rejoicing is lost, and his recreation ceases to be a pleasure.

If you don't particularly enjoy your husband's kind of recreation, you can still experience the spirit of rejoicing by encouraging him. Even when you're not together physically, your pleasure in his activities will increase his enjoyment and make him appreciate you more.

Don is an avid golfer. I've never known anyone who loves to play golf as much as he does. Don can enjoy the game with abandon because He knows he has my full support in it. I am delighted when he has time to play. We rejoice together when he is able to be out on the golf course on a beautiful day.

When he has time for recreation, Don is better able to lead our family spiritually. It helps him to unwind and get a fresh perspective on situations at work and at home. It gives him something to look forward to—something he can do just for the fun of it! It brings extra joy into his life, and joy is a great strength in marriage.

God's Word says, *"The joy of the LORD is* [our] *strength"* (Nehemiah 8:10). Joy strengthens us physically and spiritually.

Don and I frequently receive comments—even from strangers—on the joy they see in our relationship. Joy comes from the heart, and it shows on our faces. Part of that joy is the result of having learned the value of rejoicing.

Dear heavenly Father,

Help me to understand the importance of rejoicing in my marriage. Help me not to get so serious about living that I lose my perspective and forget to stop and rejoice in the beauty of Your creation. Lord, I am believing You to help me find new ways to increase my husband's joy, so we can be stronger together. In Jesus' mighty name, Amen.

10
Your Heart Shows

*I*f the message of this book could be summa-rized in one sentence, it would be: your heart shows. In every personal relationship, your heart shows. In marriage, because of the closeness of the relationship, it shows even more. Everything in this book deals with your heart in some way because God's Word says, *"Keep thy heart with all diligence; for out of it are the issues of life"* (Proverbs 4:23). Out of your heart springs the substance of your marriage.

We often try to put into practice all kinds of plans and programs to improve our marriage while our hearts remain untouched. A woman wrote to me saying she felt her husband was not attentive enough sexually. It was obvious from her letter that bitterness had developed in her heart against her husband because she felt he wasn't meeting her needs. She had a genuine problem—one that God wanted to deal with—but her plan for progress left her feeling even more dispirited. She made the common mistake of trying to evoke a change in her marriage without making a change in her heart.

This woman bought some sexy nightwear and tried to create a seductive atmosphere in their home. One day after work, she even attempted to whisk her husband away to a motel! She did everything but change her heart. All her actions served only to make him feel more pressured. The underlying statement was loud and clear to him: "Your lovemaking is a real disappointment to me. I am not satisfied with your responsiveness." It was the same criticism he had heard for years, only now it was wrapped in a different package. Her attempts to disguise her heart didn't fool her husband for a minute.

The inevitable result of trying to change your marriage without changing your heart is frustration, discouragement, and disappointment. Why? Because your heart shows.

I have seen many marriages healed, strengthened, and renewed by God, but I have never seen it happen without a heart-change first. In testimonies of transformed marriages, a similar thread is found: one partner has said, "I determined to love him/her as unto the Lord whether he/she ever changed or not."

Another term used to describe this heart-change is "unconditional love." Unconditional love is the God-kind of love—seeing your mate as God sees him or her.

Fainting Hearts

Even in the best marriages, there are times when we want to despair, to faint spiritually, or to lose our courage. In a marriage where difficulties seem to be the norm, it is doubly hard. Paul spoke of these times in Galatians 6:9: *"Let us not be weary in well doing: for in due season we shall reap, if we faint not."* Fainting has to do with losing heart and with losing our courage to go on.

Do you remember Aunt Pittypat Hamilton, the fainthearted character in *Gone with the Wind*? In those days, it was acceptable for women to "get the vapors" in an uncomfortable or embarrassing situation. To have the vapors meant a woman was about to faint or despair to the point of collapsing. I can think of many times in my own life when I would have loved to be able to "get the vapors"!

While women no longer get the vapors or faint in public, it is not unusual to see marital hearts fainting. The phrasing of their despair sounds something like this, "I had just had all I could take"; "I was tired of the marriage"; "There wasn't any love left"; "I wanted to think of myself for a change rather than always being his wife and their mother."

These women have grown weary of doing well, and in their despair they have allowed a lie to come into their hearts. The lie says that marriage is just a personal matter between the two people involved. *But history proclaims that the family unit is the very basis of society.* There has never been a nation that has survived the breakdown of the family. An ignorance of history and of God's plan for families is revealed in flippant remarks like, "A good divorce is better than a bad marriage."

The breakdown of each marriage unit has a direct and detrimental effect on hundreds of people. Schools, teachers, and classrooms are affected each time there is a divorce. Neighborhoods are shaken, and friendships are scarred.

Divorce affects other family members when beloved aunts or uncles are ripped out of the picture. The wonderful nurturing support of parents and grandparents is replaced by the grossly inadequate "step-parent" or "blended family" systems.

We are right on when we say these children come from "broken homes." *Broken* means to be reduced to fragments, to be weakened in strength or spirit. When something is broken, it is no longer complete. It has been violated. A broken home is a home that has been violated, fragmented, and weakened. My own children have been hurt deeply by divorce in our extended family. Although our marriage is strong, they have felt the loss of treasured relationships when hearts grew faint and lost courage.

Courage to Be Committed

Courage, in the selfless sense, isn't a very popular subject anymore. But there are times in marriage when nothing will replace the courage to keep going when everything in you wants to lose hope. Courage puts the needs of others above your own. Courage is a quality of mind or spirit that enables a person to face difficulty or pain with firmness. It always involves being able to go beyond your own immediate needs and your own time frame.

Rare courage involves being able to project beyond one's own life span. Early American patriots gave their lives so we could live in the freedom that is our heritage today. They were able to project their hearts and spirits beyond their own life spans. They looked beyond their own generation and their immediate family to glimpse God's timetable of eternity. They changed our world by their extraordinary courage.

We have the opportunity to change our world by showing great courage in our marriages. The world may never take note of your courage, but God never misses it.

God greatly values courage. When the Lord sent Joshua out to take the promised land, He told him three times, *"Be strong and of a good courage"* (Joshua 1:6). (See also Joshua 1:7, 9.)

The Bible speaks often of the *"mighty men of valour"* (See, for example, Joshua 1:14; 6:2; 8:3; 10:7; Judges 3:29; 18:2; 20:44, 46.) God called Gideon a *"mighty man of valour"* (Judges 6:12) and used him to deliver Israel. Courage was so important to God that He sent 32,000 of Gideon's armed men home because they were fearful and afraid. (See Judges 7.)

People exhibit rare courage in many ways. To raise a handicapped child, for example, takes tremendous courage. Such commitment requires parents with an ability to look beyond themselves, their own lives, and their own needs.

James Dobson, the well-known psychologist and radio personality, often reads on his program a letter his father wrote to his mother before they were married. The letter exhibits tremendous courage. It speaks of his commitment to her and to the marriage into which they would be entering. Dobson's father told his wife-to-be that he was committed to their future together even if things didn't work out as they planned. Even if there were difficulties greater than they could foresee, he was ready to pledge himself to her and to their marriage.

Dr. Dobson's father indicated the seriousness with which he would repeat the traditional wedding vows, "for better, for worse; for richer, for poorer; in sickness and in health." We all want the "better," the "richer," and the "health." This is what God wants for us, too, but every marriage will experience some of the "worse," some of the "poorer," and some of the "sickness" spoken of in our vows. These times call for courage.

This letter obviously had a profound effect on James Dobson's own life and marriage. He has never forgotten it. It exemplifies the courage of one's convictions, and there can be times in marriage when this is all we have to stand on.

Hope Deferred

The Bible says, *"Hope deferred maketh the heart sick"* (Proverbs 13:12), and it is so true. When we lose hope, we have lost something powerful and precious. Sometimes in marriage, we can lose hope in our relationship because we feel we no longer love our mate. We believe that when love is gone, it is gone, and that it can never be the same again. We foresee endless years of emptiness, unfulfilled dreams, and a wasted life.

Have you ever thought you lost something that could not be replaced? Modern technology has developed a way to recover lost material. When I write, I use a word processor. My thoughts are typed out on a keyboard and recorded on a floppy disk. Once in a while, I have a problem with a floppy disk, and it appears that a chapter I have just written has been lost. What a terrible feeling to think that all those hours of labor and inspiration are gone forever!

In reality, though, they are usually not lost. I have something called a recovery disk, which I can use to reprogram my machine. I can then put in a brand new floppy disk and recover the material that appeared to be erased.

God said His Word *"shall not return unto me void, but it shall accomplish that which I please, and it shall prosper in the thing whereto I sent it"* (Isaiah 55:11). As you apply the marriage principles from God's Word presented in this book, you, too, can recover something very precious that you perhaps feared had been lost forever: love for your mate.

There was a time in our marriage when I had very little feeling for my husband. I thought my love for Don was gone forever and that it could never be recovered. I had that same sinking feeling that I get when I see pages disappear from the screen of my word processor! Something precious and wonderful was lost—something I thought could never be replaced.

Perhaps you are feeling right now in your own marriage that the love is gone and that your feelings are irreversible. When I believed that love was gone, my heart was sick from deferred hope. I thought love was something you either had or did not have. I thought love came from within me, and when the well was dry, that was it. But I had forgotten the most vital aspect of love: *"God is love"* (1 John 4:8, 16). He has an unlimited supply of this precious commodity!

I don't think I need to explain the love that I feel for Don now. As I read over what I have written in this book, I find that my love for my husband is shown on every page. I feel blessed beyond measure to have Don as my husband. I am so thankful for what we have now because I know how far God has brought us. I know He was the One who poured fresh life into our marriage from a well that will never run dry. Our life together has been like the path of the just that *"shineth more and more unto the perfect day"* (Proverbs 4:18).

I had always heard that it took two to make a marriage work, but I thought the two were Don and me. What a joy to discover that God and I were enough to profoundly affect my marriage.

May this book plant hope in your heart if you have lost hope. May it help to increase your vision beyond your immediate situation if you are in despair. May you be able to stand with courage until your hope is restored. May you truly become one heart, one flesh, and one love!

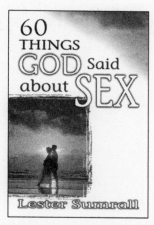

ANOTHER POWERFUL BOOK
from Whitaker House

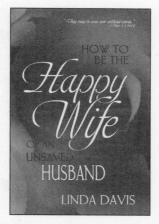

How to Be the Happy Wife of an Unsaved Husband
Linda Davis

The Christian wife of an unsaved husband has a special ministry that no one else can fulfill. Linda Davis explains how to minister to your husband while living a rewarding life both spiritually and personally. Discover how you can release your husband to God, deal with rejection and hostility, understand your husband's point of view, rely on God's perfect timing, and be happy in spite of your circumstances!

ISBN: 0-88368-358-X • Trade • 176 pages